THE ART OF
SLEEPING ALONE

WHY ONE FRENCH WOMAN
SUDDENLY GAVE UP SEX

SOPHIE FONTANEL

Translated by

LINDA COVERDALE

SCRIBNER

New York London Toronto Sydney New Delhi

SCRIBNER
A Division of Simon & Schuster, Inc.
1230 Avenue of the Americas
New York, NY 10020

Copyright © 2011 by Editions Robert Laffont, S.A., Paris.
Translation copyright © 2013 by Linda Coverdale
Originally published as *L'envie* in 2011 in France by Robert Laffont.

All rights reserved, including the right to reproduce this
book or portions thereof in any form whatsoever. For information,
address Scribner Subsidiary Rights Department,
1230 Avenue of the Americas, New York, NY 10020.

First Scribner hardcover edition August 2013

SCRIBNER and design are registered trademarks of
The Gale Group, Inc., used under license by
Simon & Schuster, Inc., the publisher of this work.

For information about special discounts for bulk purchases,
please contact Simon & Schuster Special Sales at
1-866-506-1949 or business@simonandschuster.com.

The Simon & Schuster Speakers Bureau can bring authors to your
live event. For more information or to book an event, contact the
Simon & Schuster Speakers Bureau at 1-866-248-3049 or visit our
website at www.simonspeakers.com.

Designed by Kyle Kabel

Manufactured in the United States of America

1   3   5   7   9   10   8   6   4   2

Library of Congress Cataloging-in-Publication Data is available.

ISBN 978-1-4516-9627-1
ISBN 978-1-4516-9629-5 (ebook)

The people and events described in this memoir reflect composites
and/or have been created by the author to best convey her experiences.

THE ART OF
SLEEPING ALONE

For a long while, and I really don't wish to say when it was or how many years it lasted, I chose to live in what was perhaps the worst insubordination of our times: I had no sex life. It is true that those years were in large part filled with sensuality, when dreams alone gratified my longings, but what dreams! And if I felt drawn to anything, it was only in my thoughts, but what thoughts. . . .

I realize now what that life was made of: a life in no way insignificant; on the contrary, it was rich, a perfect match for my body and myself. Yet nothing was simple, and these words I write would once have seemed leaden to me, so ashamed was I at times of my singularity, a strangeness worse than difference. Everyone knows that even people who are different have a certain sexuality worthy of the name, things to show for it, defeats they can lay claim to. Whereas we, the loners, an army that does violence only to itself, a small tribe, unavowable and hence unknowable in number, we understand instinctively that speaking out will allow the world to send us deeper into exile—and foster the kind of stupid nonsense people say about whatever they cannot comprehend. They turn us into scapegoats who reassure all others on this point: however problematic their carnal pleasures might be, we offer proof, through our most definite exclusion, that their circumstances are still better than nothing.

From this nothing, which was wholesome for me and taught me to draw upon unsuspected resources; from what a caress means to someone who no longer receives or (very likely) bestows any; from the obsession that swells within you and goes to your head; from that meek, submissive crowd I sense is out there, those whom I recognize instantly and for whom I feel such tender affection; from all this, I wanted to make a book.

I

With my elbows propped on the safety bar of the lift chair, I was raised up to where I just knew the sky would be blue, with fog slipping away like a skin skimmed from milk. I was looking at fir trees, mountaintops, immaculate planes of solid colors, and I was thinking: I want to find this calm for myself. As for the kind I'd already evaluated from personal experience, meaning the matchless scouring performed by sex, well, that no longer interested me. I'd had it with being taken and rattled around. I'd had it with handing myself over. I'd said yes too much. I hadn't taken into account the tranquility my body required.

Realizing that I wasn't listening, my body had begun to speak up. Before this winter getaway, a certain resistance had intensified within me. In the privacy of my body, every atom of my being was walling itself off, yet I couldn't do a thing about it. I had trouble unclenching my fists and strained to open my palms flat against the sheet, only to have them curl shut an instant later. For weeks, I'd been obliged to shake my head at whatever my lover proposed. He was growing impatient. I made an effort. This lover thought I was giving when

I was actually conceding. He believed I was capitulating when I was really calculating how to end the experience as quickly as possible. I'd become a paltry possession for the man who thought he had me in his power. I noticed his air of suspicion; he grew less and less sure of his spoils. He reminded me of those people who try to grab you in a fight but wind up holding your sweater while you race off, arms flailing.

I had run, run, to reach the ski resort. As soon as I got there, I bought a ski suit instead of just pants; I felt safe inside an outfit that was so hard to get off. The hotel was at the very top of the ski lift; when that stopped running at four in the afternoon, the place became a high-plains desert. It was the off-season: there were three of us at the hotel, including the owner, Jonas. My host had worshipped Johnny Hallyday ever since he was a kid, and as he served me he was listening to "Longing," his pop idol's 1986 hit. "The mountain saps self-confidence," Jonas remarked, as if to put me on my guard.

He couldn't have cared less about the fresh air. He complained about not meeting any women at such a high altitude, and going out for the evening required taking the snowmobile and coming back up again later in complete darkness, ten times more alone, drunk, and frozen stiff. His frustration amazed me. Personally, I thought it was delightful to be far from other people. And to sing about longing only for the horizon. To have the creaking of snow for my sole companion. Jonas saw things differently. He'd had no female company for three years. "I'm turning into a goat," he said, adding three logs—more than necessary—to the fireplace. Such roaring blazes were his revenge on monotony. He paid me a few compliments that first evening. Proof, suddenly, of our isolation. Tanned, athletic, Jonas was a former *chasseur alpin*, a soldier in the elite mountain infantry of the French army, and he had those pale eyes mountain folk tend to have. Untouched by the elements, the skin below his neck was white, and if I'd wanted I could have had a closer look; he would certainly have shown me. When it occurred to me—a reflex—that going to bed with this man might be a possibility, the mere thought sent my body into lockdown. It was out of the question: my whole being was slamming shut. I remembered the time I was doing a crossword puzzle in *Le Monde* and had such trouble coming up with the word "portcullis." At that moment, though, it popped right into my head.

I left Jonas and went off to my room. I thought about Paris, and what I'd escaped from, and that evening's escape as well. I opened the window onto the blackness I knew was so white. I breathed. . . . With the snow all around, my destiny seemed to me like an Eden sweet with birdsong. My life would be soft and fluffy. I was through with being had.

Those who set themselves free have the whole universe before them. I've seen it happen to people in their nineties. If I think back to my teenage years, I can see that I was like that: behind my appearance of obedience was the impulse to run away. The classes I skipped, the heady feeling that gave me! It seems crazy to compare sexuality to the servitude of school, and I know such notions of boredom, homework, the drudgery of lessons, and the tyranny of power will present a poor picture of the girl I turned out to be. We live in a culture in which people would die rather than admit to having felt listless about sex at one point in their lives. This lack of interest is often confused with impotence. A great many of us know that it isn't that we can't, it's that we can't see ourselves sticking with it. After the pleasure payoff—then what? Yesterday's imperative has faded; the game's no longer worth the candle. That's why we wander off.

I'd even claim it does a world of good.

After my snow retreat, my scrunched-up face relaxed in a matter of weeks. I know myself, and it couldn't have been the fresh air alone. Proof: in Paris, once the other benefits of the mountain had worn off, not only did I keep that face, but my appeal increased. In a photo, I discovered that I'd begun to glow. What encounter had so transfigured me? To what rendezvous was I hastening, eyes shining with confidence, skin radiant with newfound freedom? When my lover met me in a café one last time to attempt the impossible, he found this brightness more disagreeable than anything I could have said. The man could see it: my backbone was much straighter. His frown told me that he didn't know whether to consider me from now on more dangerous than a virgin, or possibly autistic, under lock and key in spite of my new, affable face— or gravitating toward another man, which would have explained everything. He checked me out from head to toe, took ten seconds to evaluate my metamorphosis, and then—it was the only solution he could think of—asked me if I was in love.

He wasn't the only one to wonder about that. After watching me sail sunnily into the café in my seven-league boots, my friend Henrietta wanted to know: "What's his name?" As soon as you've found yourself, others start trying to guess who the new person is.

I know who it was, the one for whom I was leaving everything: the girl I'd been years before. At thirteen, she looked sixteen. That girl had been given the gift of reading and would become a writer, but for the moment that was not what preoccupied her: she was dreaming of lust. A man's open shirt, especially if he had blue eyes, or that place where men have what women have in a different and unseen way—such things unsettled her. In her light summer dress, she was precocious. She assumed that we learn nothing about the senses, such knowledge being innate, and she was an adolescent bursting with impatience, eager to undergo a confirmation quite unlike that dull one in church. There had to be elevations a damn sight more esoteric. In the meantime, she studied herself in the mirror. Given her lack of perfection, she knew she was lucky to be tall and slim. What she didn't know: one of her peculiarities was the hint of darkness in her eyes. And men recognized that darkness. Men recognized what was askew in that girl. What was his name, that chance encounter, a honey-tongued tourist from Mexico with the curly hair of an archangel? *Tus ojos,* he said to her: "Your eyes . . ." It was in a nightclub that should never have let her in at her age, of course. Not that she would have been allowed out, at that point.

They'd seen each other again the next day; he wanted to go to a museum. This interest in culture made her feel safer, and her chatter positively sparkled. He had to swing by his hotel, but she didn't mind seeing a palace. It was near the famous church La Madeleine. He took off some of his clothes, just for fun. That guy's perfect sweet-as-sugar torso . . . He liked the Impressionists, and he was handsome. Fascinated, she was hopeful. He'd taken off the rest of his clothes: he was naked, and the gaiety reached its zenith. This really was what she'd always had in mind. It was fabulous. No need to worry about it anymore: one day, everything would happen. At thirteen, ecstatic at such favorable signs, she wanted to leave it at that. To rest secure in that knowledge for a few years. She started to get out of the bed. The guy grabbed her wrist. She said she wanted to leave. He laughed in a stupid, bad-boy way. He was twenty years older than she was. "I'm really thirteen," she protested. For all her intelligence, she was ridiculously naïve. Because—what was she thinking? That a man at such a pitch of desire, a stranger who would go back home to his own country the next day, would pause for a discussion?

We were fifteen, Henrietta and I. She was the best student in school. Destined for a shining career as an archaeologist, she would later sashay around the ancient necropolis of Alexandria for the BBC. We were lounging on her wicker bed in her parents' apartment, cramming for a Latin exam, and had just finished doing Greek. Henrietta loved studying so much that she could almost speak the dead languages that constantly tripped me up, and I can see her now, tracking the cryptic texts of Livy with her fingertips, deciphering them as she went. To her they were a familiar braille, and on that day, she was barreling along through a translation of the Second Punic War. Perhaps she was poking fun at me over some genitive case I had muffed. Henrietta didn't have a mean bone in her body, but she simply reveled in knowing more than other people. So I decided to show her a thing or two. Setting aside my Latin book, just to indicate that we were shifting fields of expertise, I told her point-blank that I'd been with a man.

The effect was even more than I'd hoped for. Henrietta was perfectly aware that the supremacy of Latin had its limits when compared with live bodies. Besides, she was myopic, wore glasses, and had a complex about her Coke-bottle lenses. An awkward adolescent, she didn't shine in that department. Leaning her still-skimpy chest close to me, she murmured, "Tell me."

It disconcerted me to have the advantage. "You don't want to tell me?" she asked anxiously, afraid I might decide to keep this trumpeted secret. Now that I'd produced my effect, what would be the most powerful ploy, the most radical counterweight to Latin: talking, or clamming up? As I pondered the problem, the temptation to confide in at least one person, a vital human necessity equal to our most basic needs, became overwhelming. For the first time I described in detail the Mexican accent, the visit to the museum, the hotel near the Madeleine. I spoke of how attractive men's bodies were, the softness of the skin on their backs and in other places, and their cruel indifference to our fears and apprehensions. As for the act itself, racing ahead of Henrietta's legitimate curiosity, I informed her that the closer a man got, the more uncontrollable he became. Past a certain point, he spoke without the slightest consideration for his partner, who in any case no longer dared to ask for any.

One confides more than one suspects. Henrietta was so silent that I panicked and quickly insisted that I had, after all, actively desired such an encounter. It was life, and I, well, I had discovered the hidden part of it. The part about which our parents were warning us with their silences, their horrified sign language, and their prohibitions against going out. *They* knew what great truth marked the end of childhood.

I was twenty and I had my first serious boyfriend. In spite of the many pleasures he'd known before I came along, he considered me irreplaceable. He loved the way I could be awakened in the middle of the night without getting grumpy. In bed he could waggle my head back and forth in his hands, and even with my hair every which way, I still didn't bat an eye. He loved the power he felt. He gloried in putting me through my paces: it fed his pride. He had taken to striding around his apartment like a king. Still, no matter how he boasted of his conquest, whenever he asked me to work my hint of darkness on him, that was enough to turn the tables straightaway. We'd play at staring into each other's eyes and see who could last the longest without laughing, but he always wound up making a joke of it to hide the way my impassivity disturbed him.

One day, I'd just returned from a class at the Sorbonne. My boyfriend was in bed watching one of those absurd afternoon TV programs, a show about dog handlers. A colonel in the fire department was saying that the "trickiest" dogs are not the ones the public thinks. During an intervention, the dog that barks at you seems the most fearsome. It isn't. From ten yards away, it broadcasts how dangerous it is to someone it can't reach, someone who has time to plan an approach, establish a relationship with the animal. The dog that seems entirely placid, on the other hand, simply wagging its tail, the one that doesn't growl when you're five yards or a few inches away, will stick out a friendly muzzle, greet the palm of your hand with a moist nose, roll over on its back, close its eyes if you scratch the top of its head, enjoy being patted, let you get close enough for a sniff so that your face is in its brown fur; you can hold up its jowls to make a silly smile, you happen to touch some nondescript place on its spine—and this dog whips around to tear off your cheek.

The photo of one of these tricky dogs appeared, a female Dalmatian. Considering what we'd just learned, the animal's friendliness seemed chilling. My boyfriend remarked that it was unbelievable, that nothing distinguished this female from other dogs. Its handsome spotted coat made you think of a favor bestowed. There seemed no explanation for why such a young and lovely creature would hate human beings. My boyfriend leaned back on the pillows. "Luckily she's not my dog!" He patted the bed where I was to join him. I felt some misgivings. As soon as I had seen the Dalmatian, I'd realized that that female was me.

After my winter interlude, I continued to escape Paris. I couldn't stop looking for fresh air. During one of these trips, down near Manosque, a typical Provençal town in southeastern France, on a morning that seemed full of promise, I learned that a craftswoman living not far from the village where I was staying sold virgin wool. I was convinced that I needed some. We set off, my body and I, riding lightly in our convertible.

I couldn't find the woman's farmhouse. The country roads I was on kept leading me to tumbledown walls. The last road climbed a hill to a high plateau and stopped at a field of poppies. Thwarted in my desire to reach the farmhouse and the wool, I felt foolishly discouraged. The slightest obstacle was enough to demoralize me. When you're on the run, even the tiniest hindrance assumes dramatic proportions, fueled by your fear of recapture. I needed to feel all-powerful, believing it to be a requirement for disentangling myself from the schemes of men. Nothing ought ever to cross my will again. What is freedom, if you don't have what you want? On I drove, determined. I did not like having my route turn into a dead end. It all came back to me: you can erase things, they fade, but in a certain light, that writing becomes legible once more.

I'd botched and imprisoned my desire for a long time. As for the hotel episode near the Madeleine, I could assume that I'd been thoughtless, careless. But afterward, when I kept pledging allegiance in every direction? My poor envelope of flesh was always there, and when it lost, the loss was grievous. The constant discomforts of those years came to mind: instead of changing course, I had backaches, I'd get sick, was always tired. Warning signs. Once, a doctor had spoken to me, squinting up from under beetling brows as if addressing someone other than myself, someone more concerned and inclined to pay attention to him: "People should listen to their bodies." My heart had ricocheted around against my ribs. I didn't understand what he was insinuating, this doctor who had just spent forty minutes (twice as long as for his other patients) examining me. From appointment to appointment, he played the conciliator between my envelope and me. For weeks he would take care of me. As soon as I felt a smidgen better, I'd go back to forgetting myself. I was ready to be banged into again.

Could it trust me, this body, after the rough treatment I'd put it through? The answer was not long in coming: a cramp in one thigh drove me out of the car and into the poppy field to stretch my legs. My feet vanished into thousands of flowers, thousands of bees. I kept moving toward the horizon, impelled by some kind of energy, and soon I was in the midst of the poppies. The cramp was gone; my body now hummed with repose. We finally formed a single perfect insect.

II

When was I ever happier than during those first few months of respite? I took lavender milk baths. The Japanese sell a perfumed powder that turns the water white. Pouring the contents of the sachet into the bathtub, reveling in that unctuous liquid and then sinking into it, I felt as if some divinity were rejoicing for me. Until then, water had been only a useful element, like the showers, for example, into which I rushed to cleanse myself of a presence after having let myself be caught. The soap attenuated the repercussions of every "no" and "later" left unspoken, as well as my constantly compromised fastidiousness. I'd spend an inordinate time in the little shower stall, leaning back against the tiles, from exhaustion.

But now, except for my head, I was immersed in milk. My body, relaxed, would agree to float, and its most meaningful parts would emerge from the opaline water, my breasts upthrust like buoys signaling a human presence along a seacoast. I was beneath these beacons, a living being. And soon the détente would continue as the other important part of my anatomy would rise, no longer mistreated as before. The palm of a sorcerer had slid beneath my hips to gently raise me. Even today, on an anatomical drawing I could still trace with my finger the circuit of freedom flowing through my body in those limpid moments. I was confident. I rejoiced at being out of all danger. They weren't going to get me. They weren't going to get anything from me. If levitating is something real, then that's what it was.

At night, I would hug my pillow, exactly as if it were a human being. I treated it with the care you take with someone you would never wish to harm. I cherished it; anyone trying to take it would have had to tear it from my arms. Dare I say that I embraced it? I was entrusting myself to the back of an imaginary man, resting my forehead between his shoulder blades, wrapping my arms around him as he held my hands in his own. He moved slowly, and so little that I could have sworn he was merely breathing. It took me some time to understand that he was rocking me. How did he manage his own desire? I had no idea. My only desire was to wait. Perhaps the man would turn around, and his vastness would cover me. For the moment, though, I was in no danger.

It was happiness. And we know that happiness makes us look all around for ways to share it. And so, absorbed in the intoxication of my discovery, I saw no reason not to talk about it. I confided in Axel, a friend of my parents, with whom I had a special relationship. He had been the rare adult, in my childhood, to take seriously my determination to become a writer. The rare one to urge me to do things on my own. And even if he was talking about me traveling by myself at the time, now it was definitely a question of figuring out how to make my own way.

Axel admitted that as far as the pillow was concerned, he did the same thing. Not only did he hug his bolster, he would whisper "Malika" to it, the name of his great lost love. One day, in a moment of weakness, Axel had described to his friends what he did at night—and had encountered only pity tinged with disgust. So he was well placed to advise me against that kind of admission. His conclusion? "There are limits to what people can hear." Not one of his friends had understood him. And what's more, he had damaged his dream. Everything we scatter is lost. To others Axel was now no more than someone they no longer saw, an outcast shrouded in sheets, his body a closed circuit, tragic and convulsed.

"Listen, Axel," I said, protesting, "you're the one who taught me that a person can always and everywhere manage to break free." Now he sadly shook his head. "Believe me. We others, we're only strong if we keep quiet."

On the radio, a doctor was insisting that the more someone makes love, the better that person will become in every domain. I cracked up. My mockery had no effect on that man, who persevered in his catechism. He reminded us that the human body is a mechanism and compared it to the elevated metro line in Taipei. Years earlier, a flaw had been discovered in the construction of the concrete pillars supporting the just-completed metro line. Well, this metro had run without passengers day and night to keep it from rusting. According to the doctor, a similar constraint governed the sexual body: use it, or lose it.

Listeners could call the station to share their experiences. I dialed the number and surprisingly quickly found myself talking to an operator who asked for my comments on that day's topic. I said that I was aghast (not at the operator, obviously). I said that the redoubtable and ultramodern conventions of our time were inescapable but that, naïvely, I was nevertheless amazed to find them on a respectable radio program. I proved that it wasn't true, this business about becoming a better person by making love more often. For example:

Saint Francis of Assisi, Mother Teresa, the Dalai Lama, Buddha. And what about a companion who's been hostile and exasperating for hours, ignoring your devotion, humiliating you in front of others, cursing your very existence, who then tries to make up again at night on the cheap? You wind up having to go along with this willy-nilly—and hating him. That's good for your health, is it? I said, "Why valorize the concept of a sex life simply because it's a sex life? There are oodles of inner dispositions and exterior circumstances involved. What *would* make a person better would be not to believe a word of this doctor's canonical pronouncements." I suggested, "Leave people the treasure they possess: their indescribable equilibrium." *Indescribable,* I emphasized that. "Which, by the way, is why no word can encompass the absence of a sex life for people who are simply waiting hopefully. We say 'chastity'; that's not the right word. We say 'abstinence'; that's not the right word. 'Asexuality' is not the right word. So stop. Enough of this nonsense."

The operator was a young man, I could tell by his voice. He told me that he was sincerely sorry, but what I had to say was too complicated, they couldn't put my call directly on the air. He did hope that I had enjoyed listening to the program on that station, which was delighted to offer me, in recognition of my faithful listenership, a makeup case from Clinique.

was driving along the Seine. To my right, a low wall blocked my view of the river. To the left were the raised terraces of the Tuileries gardens. The young man startled me; passing close to me on the roadway, he had tapped the hood of my car with his fingers. A Rollerblader. He was wearing a pullover in the glacial chill of April. A big ecru Irish turtleneck. Sleeves pushed up, caramel-colored leather gloves. His hips swiveled in the too-tight jeans, but who says a skilled blader can't be a narcissist? We were both going at about the same speed, I in the flow of traffic, he thanks to the momentum he'd built up. Watching him zigzag among the vehicles, one couldn't help thinking about the risks he was taking. I thought him foolhardy, daring to weave through the traffic. What would happen if he skidded, if a moment's inattention slammed him to the pavement head over heels? His supple assurance showed me that he would have laughed off my fears. Even more important than wheels and a smooth surface, it was his absolute self-confidence that bore him along. Whenever a seriously big car came within reach, he made it tow him along on one leg. Instead of being more careful, he affirmed his aplomb, and when he let go and dropped his other foot to the pavement, a ripple of joy went through his whole body before he wove his way toward other vehicles. When I had to stop at a light, he went on, defying the danger. To increase his speed, he had bent forward, then stretched his arms backward like the wings of a dragonfly and twirled his gloved hands to bid adieu to us all and all obligations.

In the midst of others one can dare to be different.

One afternoon in Paris, a movie. I went to the Lucernaire three times a week. There were never more than ten of us in the theater, and that day I was alone. I turned around to wave in friendly solidarity to the unseen projectionist. The film was Sydney Pollack's *Three Days of the Condor*. Robert Redford leaves his office (a clandestine CIA agency) to go get sandwiches. When he returns in his navy blue peacoat with everyone's lunch, his colleagues are dead, riddled with bullets. Redford was supposed to have been murdered with the others; his continued existence now poses a threat, so he must go into hiding. In the final freeze frame, he turns to look back over his shoulder.

There are a thousand ways to appropriate a film for yourself, but are women who can love a real man *available* enough to get to know Robert Redford? I know they take a little away from a film, get some use out of it. That's not much. For those women it's only a film. Because absent the absolute nakedness of the viewer, Robert Redford stays put. You have to be at the Lucernaire, with the double retrenchment of being in the theater and in your body (hands lying open and empty at your sides), with your imperative need to dream, you who now spend time exclusively with beauty, you for whom the film is truly a *lucernaire* (a lamp-lighting ceremony to dispel darkness), you who can make love without moving, you who (let me remind you) are now a field poppy and so need very little water to bloom, you who are seeking nourishment from Robert Redford to water yourself—well, Robert Redford? *You* he can see.

If this actor were to come over to talk to me at a party, I'd be wary. I'd wonder what he wanted from me. I believe, yes, I believe I'd even be frightened. But I was in a movie theater thousands of miles from the real body of Robert Redford. Only the essence of him remained. Disembodied, the both of us, we were resurrected in the heavenly precincts of the Lucernaire. Redford could have carried me off in the folds of his craggy complexion. That rock face of his had places that made me think, If this goes any further, that's where I'll grab a handhold.

You must believe in miracles. At the end of the film, when I was standing up in the dark as the credits were rolling, Robert Redford placed a hand on my shoulder to offer me a fourth Day of the Condor. It was only logical. He had received my message. I draped one arm around his handsome neck saved from the killers and figured that if the projectionist was watching, he'd think I was consulting my watch.

III

My father had a cousin, Charles, who was a priest and held jobs in the secular world for missionary purposes. Every summer he spent a week with us on the Côte d'Azur. He belonged to the learned order of the Dominicans. Through him came culture and the respected national newspaper *Le Monde,* which he bought when he went out to get bread. He had weighty conversations with my father, who always emerged from them with a sanctified countenance. My father was not a believer. Neither my mother, my brother, nor I ever found out what they could possibly have talked about. However, their mysterious discussions were not the most extraordinary thing about these vacations; it was that Charles strode around the port of Saint-Tropez in boxer trunks. That didn't mean anything to most people, as you couldn't tell he was a priest, but within my parents' small circle of friends, the effect was sensational. A priest in a bathing suit, a man of God endowed with a body! And that this devoted divine servant belonged to us, that he was of our blood, placed us well up in the social hierarchy at the beach. Whenever Charles was there, we became something like stars. Since our visitor's sainthood didn't stretch as far as teetotaling, his presence implied numerous predinner cocktails, during which Charles, at first quite proper, would become more and more convivial, thanks to the libations, and would wind up holding forth as the center of attention. He had so much to say, this man, a prison chaplain in the north of France, formerly a high official who had left a prestigious position with the Banque de France to go work first in the coal mines and then in a textile mill before becoming a prison chaplain. A man who still believed in humanity, while the rest of us had long since thrown in the towel. A man who never nagged anyone about God for fear of "losing the ear of atheists." To put you at ease, he set aside his faith, letting you know that it was his private concern even when it wasn't.

Why all these considerations? Poor Charles, that wasn't what his audience expected from him, and they gently nudged him toward a different subject. Each evening the aperitif hour was simply a hypocritical progression toward the important question, the one that defines a man. On the last evening, after beating at length about the bush, they would finally ask: Didn't Charles find it onerous, this lack of sexual relations? Axel—if he'd been drinking—tormented him as much as the others. And Charles, a little tight and with a mischievous gleam in his eye, would try to duck the question. Sitting in his shorts, naked (so to speak), his toes twiddling nervously in his Saint James of Compostela sandals, yet with hands clasped canonically before him, he would declare that the love of God is in itself a form of hedonism. Everyone would up the ante: yes, but a woman! Then each inquisitor in turn would approach and tap him on the thigh, emboldened by the pastis, insisting, saying good heavens, did he not see the beauty of women, did that not stir up some twinge somewhere? Did he have desires? Didn't the sins he heard about in confession give him any ideas? No? No? Had everything atrophied to the point that nothing worked anymore?

After a few months, my friends became curious about me in the same way. I was already a journalist, meeting lots of people through my profession, and I lived as part of a pack. Sometimes there were ten of us at a simple impromptu weeknight supper. And almost all of us went in pairs, so my solitude could not pass unnoticed.

One couple, Vionne and Carlos, were the most tenacious. It's incredible how much of a ruckus a couple can kick up. At first they had admired my courage; I'd been able to feel like a heroine. Those halcyon days were over. Now barely had they said hello when they'd ask if I'd found someone. I'd shake my head—and they'd pitch a fit of amazement, pressing me to explain how that was possible: Was I doing all that was necessary? They'd check out what I was wearing with a knowing air. No dress was cut deeply enough. My hair was too messy. I had to show more leg. And stop being such a pal. And the heels—why wasn't I wearing heels? Carlos had a theory that heels were the decisive index of a woman's accessibility, since no woman perched on them can take off at a run. And it's true that if I compared myself to Vionne—Vionne's long lustrous locks, Vionne's staggeringly high heels—I must admit that of the two of us, it was Vionne who attracted men, Vionne who already had one—and a Spaniard to boot.

I had noticed this when my father died: no convalescence is allowed to last too long. People tolerate your inactivity for a while, but alas, that can cease overnight. You are still grief-stricken; they have finished mourning your loss. Same thing now: my freedom had to be paired with availability, or else it became a disorder. I pleaded my cause with vigor. I certified that I was just fine, a feeble argument I attempted to shore up by alluding to Robert Redford's love for me. They were appalled. Luckily, thanks to Axel's warning, I'd kept mum about my pillow. They would have crushed me. The Redford thing alone drove them crazy.

"You're sleepwalking!" they told me, and glanced disapprovingly at my flat-heeled boots. What good would it have done me to inform Carlos that Coco Chanel had worn the same ones, that they came from Church's English Shoes (founded in 1873) in Paris, that they were bespoke (a restyling of a men's model), and that I'd waited nine months for them?

If there was a party, everyone in turn would come sit next to me to regale me with how he or she thought I should live and what I deserved to have. What it boiled down to was that I should live like them. Elvire, one half of a tightly knit couple, would forget that her husband was clinically depressed. Guillaume, married to a harpy, maintained that if one laid low and said amen to everything, things worked out. Maria, fed up to the teeth with her children, wanted me to have my own. Assia loved women but it was killing her mother. Patrizio had bruises on his shoulders from his chronically jealous wife. Not one of them could stand my singleness, because it could have been theirs. And the marginal couple, Sabine and William, doleful swingers, who absolutely had to stay together to have someone to swap—even they found me peculiar. I was discovering conventional behavior in the most liberated milieus: broad-minded people, against any form of censorship or constraint, who boasted about how they pushed boundaries. Well, I blasted them back in the other direction, and they flung their hands up. They had ingested the most useless hodgepodge of drugs, blitzing themselves so completely that they'd forgotten I'd seen them do it, whereas I was mainlining the purest of ideals, of the very highest quality—and this shocked them.

The dinner party hosted by the curator at the Musée de l'Homme, where they were so eager to introduce me to someone. . . . I'd walked in and spotted him easily: he was smoking, bristling with defiance, near an open window. He was furious in advance (I could read him perfectly) at having been instructed to come see if he might like me, instead of having it just happen. In love, it's such a drag when you're not waiting for a miracle anymore but for a mere possibility.

At dinner, seated next to me, the man felt obliged (in case I'd heard about his situation) to downplay it. "I see a little action here and there," he informed me, so that I wouldn't imagine him hugging his pillow during lonely nights without end. I had caught him chewing on a chicken drumstick he hadn't realized had been deboned, and his stupefaction when he'd nibbled it down to nothing in his hands was priceless. At the far end of the table, Henrietta was winking at me.

Since we were in the same situation, the man spoke frankly, giving me the details of his two previous adventures.

There'd been a girl from whom he'd concealed his real identity so that if she grew attached to him, she would have no way of tracking him down. And another one, nineteen years old; he'd been cautious with her as well: she was from the Horn of Africa, and undocumented. He was wary of traps and didn't see that he'd already fallen into the worst one, cynicism. He sent 2,500 euros a month to the mother of his son. It was obvious that he feared entanglements and would twist free of them whatever the cost.

When it was time to leave, there was a kind of milling about in which everyone could see that we were being pushed, that man and I, toward a bottleneck in which we'd have no other choice but to get together. I'll never forget the look on his face when I announced that I wasn't leaving. He had his coat on, had resigned himself to leaving with me, and I wasn't coming. The door shut in his face. My friends turned toward me. It was war.

We went to sit in the living room. Dear God, how docile I was. . . .

Three couples, and across from them, me. The museum curator stood over by his mantelpiece, an intellectual authority, with his own companion, a boyfriend, sitting on a pouf beside him. And they started in on me. Why hadn't I suggested to that man that we go have a drink? Why hadn't I pronounced the following formula: "I'd be delighted to see you again"? Why had I coyly played hard to get (which I'd apparently done) instead of playing hardball? How come I didn't know how simply to exercise some feline cunning? They were pouncing on me with fangs bared, and I was the animal knocked off balance.

"Leave her alone," said Henrietta. "If she doesn't feel like it . . ."

That person who didn't feel like it was welcomed into vacation homes as an extra child would be. As summer approached, Vionne had suggested, "Why don't you join us in Hydra? You must know we'll always have room for you." Hearing that magic phrase, I'd quickly forgotten my craving for rebirth, the great spreading of my wings and the world wide open at my disposal. I'd bought the plane ticket, flown to Athens, took a taxi to the port of Piraeus, bought a ticket to Hydra, and boarded the boat. Water splashed the portholes of the hydrofoil; you couldn't see outside. Inside, it was all families, groups, and people in pairs.

My friends—four couples and Henrietta—came to meet me at the dock in Hydra. The children applauded my emergence from the boat before running to fling themselves at my neck. Carlos took the suitcase from my hands. Feeling proud of being greeted by a group, I'd flashed an arrogant smile at the other passengers. We human beings are such weak things.

The house was at the top of the village. The children tried to show it to me by pointing in all different directions. I was informed that it was stupendous. It didn't have its feet in the water, it had its nose to the sky, and in that stifling summer the slightest breeze was just for us. In short, I was climbing up to Eden. A sour note was struck when I learned that there wasn't all that much space in the amazing villa. In fact, there wasn't a room for me. Far from dampening the children's good humor, this gave them fresh delight. I was going to play with them instead of staying alone in my corner. I offered to go to a hotel. No, my friends had already made inquiries: at that time of year everything was booked. Under no circumstances would I be abandoned. I would share a room with Henrietta for a few days; Pierre wouldn't arrive until the end of the week. Then I would be with Rosa, Vionne's daughter; they'd make up a bed for me. These plans were announced on the whitewashed steps of Hydra, amid ravishing houses, with the sea and the clanking masts below in the harbor. I would have the view. And my friends who loved me. The children hugged my hips. Carlos was carrying my suitcase. I thought it over quickly. What would I have done with a room of my own?

In the morning, I rose before Henrietta. The rooms gave onto an immense terrace. I didn't really know where to go without disturbing those still asleep, the couples. I took a book to a deck chair to read. The chair creaked, and I flinched. Had I made too much noise? Having suspected that I was awake, a child appeared before me holding a box of cereal. He was hungry. I rose with useless caution, since the boy galloped toward the kitchen, his feet loudly slapping the tiles. I taught him how to whisper. He thought it was a game and spoke very quietly before shrieking as shrilly as possible. The other children arrived one after another. I set the table out on the terrace. I heated milk, got out the jams. I waved bees away from the table; they frightened the children. I told them little stories from the *Odyssey*. They listened. Arm outstretched, I kept gesturing toward the vastness of Greece, my nightgown improvising flowing drapery dazzling to a child. "You're beautiful," they said. They asked me why I didn't have a lover. I told them that they were my lovers. They kissed my arms. They snuggled against my ribs. They confided secrets I will not betray, about the bad words they'd heard and the things their parents did at night. Without my asking, they began to clear the table, to prove that our understanding fostered a community. Making noise was no longer important, and now they were murmuring. "We love you," they said. I understood how, at other times—not that long ago, in fact—women had managed to insert themselves like this into families, to raise children who were not their own and succeed in assuming vital importance.

An automobile rally in the Sahara. He had brought me along. She had too much work; she couldn't travel. He had almost canceled the trip. No one wanted to accompany him during a real competition where you'd get four hours' sleep a night and sand in your hair. And then he'd thought of me. His wife had said, "With her, it's okay."

In the morning, we'd roll along singing until the car bogged down. The wheels would spin uselessly no matter which levers were shifted. We had to use the boards for getting the car out of the sand at least ten times a day. By two in the afternoon, we were exhausted. Luckily, night fell early. During the "duo" stages, we weren't supposed to join the campsite at night; it was the rule. We had to fend for ourselves. We dined on crackers and canned goods, spent hours setting up the little tent, and when it was more or less serviceable, we slipped inside, so excited after laughing so much that we weren't tired anymore.

One evening, we were lying side by side on our backs, each wrapped in our Scottish sleeping bags, the zippers pulled up to our noses. In February, nights in the Sahara are glacial.

He asked if I didn't miss it.

The crispness of the air made me want to be honest. I admitted that from time to time, I wondered about things. Did I really have a choice? My feeling was that this choice was basically to go back to men or become a child again. What else was there to do? I wouldn't have known how to say what it was I had fled, but my one conviction was the absolute refusal to go back there. So?

He listened to me. Was he listening to me? All I could hear was his steady breathing. I began to think he might have fallen asleep again in the darkness of the tent.

"Life is always hard."

I thought he was telling me this as if my having no sex life made me some kind of extraterrestrial who needed instruction in the ways of humans. But no, he was in a confiding mood. He said that bodies bound by love had their problems as well. Even he, despite his feelings and a woman to whom he had pledged his body, even he had to struggle. Some evenings, caught in the tangle of his need to be welcomed, his fear of disappointing, and real desire, he couldn't tell anymore what it was that drove him to offer words of love. He told me about evenings when he saw himself as a wild animal. Going home, he would imagine terrible escape fantasies. A double life: he would be a spy, one who could allow himself all sorts of delinquencies. And he recognized his own sexual hunger lurking behind this shadowy profession, which was simply an alibi.

On the way home from work he would roam through the woods of Meudon, just southwest of Paris, where the transvestites gathered, his mind churning with carnal projects that never went anywhere, because he'd wind up back home without really remembering how he'd gotten there. "You're handling it pretty well," he told me in the tent. He'd leave it at that. Otherwise, given the perfect silence, they'd have been able to hear us way out in Meudon, where his love was waiting.

This guy, he had been a star. Now he came alone in the evenings to this expensive restaurant at the Palais-Royal, where he sat at a secluded table reserved for him. In a way, he was still performing for a public: the entire room witnessed his meal of melancholy. The people I was with that evening knew him. We stopped by. He gestured toward the empty chairs around him, a desert more arid than the Sahara: "Would you like to join me?" Although he was speaking to us all, it was my arm he tugged, as if it were an old velvet bellpull. He appropriated women with a nod of his head. My companions were disconcerted, and I was of two minds as well. What did I have, in my "retreat," that could interest such a man? Leaning toward me, he asked quietly what I was doing with these people, as if I deserved better. That disparagement hinted at how few friends he had, since even the ones I was with—whom he'd invited to sit down—didn't make the cut. I replied that one can't say no to everything and that these friends helped to entertain me. He asked me right away if I was a very solitary person. I couldn't decide if he had guessed that or if he hoped it was true and meant to marry me. Once you stop

making love, fairy tales become real. I had no more needs—
and the unexpected would simply happen to me. One day
such things come to seem normal to a dreamer.

"I'm quite alone," I ventured to say. "And you?"

"Oh," he said with a sigh, "me, no one." And added,
"Luckily, I have a Monet. . . ."

I knew exactly what kind of sublimation he meant. I saw
art as a refuge and planned to live in it (sans Monet) with my
books, good films, music. I gave a gentle, comradely shoulder
bump to that man. He hugged me, careful to explain to the
others that he'd taken a liking to me. I had just learned that
one great loneliness always knows how to speak to another
one.

He left us on the sidewalk outside the restaurant. Hardly
had his distinguished and brutal back moved off down the
street than everyone piped up with an anecdote. The habits
of that handsome man and the inventory of his male and
female lovers were run through in a few minutes. It's jaw-
dropping what people dare to divulge about the private lives
of others.

IV

Henrietta used to say I was a mirror. She would stand next to me with her arms at her sides, looking my reflection in the eye, head craned forward, comparing her mystery with mine. I didn't dare move a muscle, afraid to damage some aspect of this candid intimacy. Unlike me, she was born to draw close to others and be constructive; even her gift for dead languages was part of her penchant for proximity, and she insisted to me that my existence calmed her and that I was right to give myself a breather.

She'd been the first of my friends to bind herself to a man through love: Pierre, a law student at the time, moved in with her at nineteen and settled into her life. She'd been the first to accept the consequences of that. She willingly agreed that the body of another person is an encumbrance, but that did not alter her consent in the least. She had figured out earlier than most that without anything, one has nothing. And it was Henrietta, the complete conformist, who on her own approached my difference with a joyous complicity, coaxing me along from the sidelines of the tribe.

Well, one day when we were at the Turkish baths, my

friend turned her dripping face to me and asked, "How long is it now that you've had nothing?" Nothing? I couldn't get over it: she of all people asking me that. I reminded her that I levitated and that Robert Redford loved me. Wiping away the droplets, she replied briskly, "You can't call delusion pleasure." That made me wonder what *she* called pleasure. Alas, I wasn't in a position to quibble, because Henrietta was already calculating on her fingers how indecently long my austerity had lasted. She counted twice, too, to give me a second chance, in case she'd been mistaken. She was returning to reality, and my ecstasies, my dear ecstasies, were falling apart. I felt like the class simpleton who thinks she has aced the essay and then the teacher reads her paper and crosses out half the words. It's a sad thing when someone you love doesn't follow you. And what was she trying to teach me by calling my delicate balance into question? Nothing had changed since our Latin days; I was incapable of making progress.

As abruptly as she had begun tormenting me, she told me, "Forget what I just said."

The place was called Monster Park. The entrance fee permitted children to dash off to slides, climb walls, go on swings and tilt-a-whirls, and to shout, "Mama!" from every one of them. Even off on their own, they craved attention. Sitting next to me, she had to rise and applaud her children. She complained of being harassed by their demands. On the other hand, if she didn't hear them, she stood up, fearing she'd lost them.

We'd become acquainted at our university. Now she lived in Basel, light-years away from our former routines on the rue des Écoles and the film series of the Cinémathèque Française. She was impeccably turned out, with a designer handbag instead of the messy treasure trove of former days. She'd married an industrialist, an expert in biotechnology. Just as I was thinking that it probably wasn't much fun living in Basel, she began extolling the wonderful sex life she enjoyed with her husband. Some folks in Basel got up to serious high jinks, so to speak. In fact this couple was possessed. The industrialist's penis was like an insatiable doll: although loath to omit a single detail, she had to give up on a complete catalog of its triumphs; there were simply too many. "We never stop," she said. She found sex to be such a natural thing. Like breathing. This attraction she felt for these pleasures came from a real gift she had: her talent for coming. In Basel she would go out onto her balcony, caress the wood of the railing, and thank heaven for her sensuality, her appreciation for saliva, clotted cream, juices, and bodies. She bought herself sexy underwear in a London store I'd doubtless never heard of. She'd take both tops and bottoms: ensembles were prettier. She went through the tops quickest; they stretched out because the industrialist pulled on them so much. She had too many silk culottes and would bring me some the next time she was in Paris.

Although she couldn't have been more fulfilled, still, she did have a hankering for other men. She had spent years hiding certain dreams from her companion. She'd been wrong. When she had made up her mind to put her cards on the table, the results were gratifying. The industrialist had adored this idea of expressing one's desires and had revealed his own fantasies, among which was a threesome with another woman. He would imagine his wife and this woman making love, and then he would make love to them, and this way everyone would have made love. My old acquaintance had acquired a taste for that scenario. I shouldn't take it personally, but I was the one they imagined most in the extra role. They would focus on my modesty, my timid refusal. . . . It galvanized them.

She was one of the gang; that's how I knew her. A night owl. I didn't go out much, but whenever I was flagging and ready to leave, she would show up. She always exclaimed at seeing me, as if that were the best surprise of the evening, running into me. "Leaving already?" she'd ask. At four in the morning.

She had obtained my phone number. I couldn't pretend this meeting wasn't important because after all, she had asked for it a week in advance, babbling nervously on the phone. Sitting in front of me, she was a striking girl: perfect posture, breasts molded by the tight sweater. Her ponytail high, her face bare of makeup save for the scarlet mouth.

In her eyes, that hint of darkness.

Her hands flat on the Formica table of the café, she had come to tell me this: "I envy you." She wished to express her respect for my solution of doing without men. As soon as she'd learned what I was living without, she had started thinking about confiding in me. It had taken months for her to actually call me. "You impress me," she said. Hungarian. Her French was excellent. She had studied geography in Paris, she lived in Brussels, she'd been working at the European Council for a year now. She was going to make it. She'd worked wonders to get out of her country, but that hadn't been her only obstacle. She had other things to leave behind. Men had preyed on her since her adolescence. Her hips and breasts had developed early, signaling the end of a certain equilibrium. For as far back as she could remember, she'd let herself be swept up by men. She would adapt to the feelings that arose. But . . . it brought her a pleasure to which she was basically indifferent. At the age of sixteen, in the Hungarian city of Debrecen, boys would pummel her with compliments by the lake near her home, and she'd sensed that one day she would become fed up with being the apple of men's eyes. And as for men, she now felt she'd pretty much exhausted that subject. It had taken her a while to admit that to herself. She was aware that most of the time one kept quiet for the simple reason that once you've admitted something, there's no longer any excuse not to move on.

I wanted to know why she was telling me all this. "Because I'm like you," she replied. I asked if I could help in any way. She made a furtive movement to one side—her breasts inside her sweater loomed a little larger—and I saw her scarlet mouth zoom toward my lips. I instinctively protected my face. The mouth was so full and heavily lipsticked that my thumbnail sank into it during this defensive maneuver. My tea spilled all over me. She tried to sponge it up with a napkin.

She had thought that since I wasn't seeing men anymore, I would go for a woman.

At the café Le Bonaparte, I had just told Axel about the spilled tea. "What a misunderstanding, what a misunderstanding," I kept saying. I felt guilty about my violent reaction.

Axel had heard me out while munching on peanuts. I was waiting for his opinion to jibe with mine, which was usually the case. But, in disagreement with our agreements, as he handed the empty bowl to the waiter he asked me, "And what if you liked women?" He studied me with passionate intensity, as if there were some secret to winkle out. Axel had known me since childhood. He had taught me to swim, and one day had taken off my float wings and made me believe that he had his hand under my tummy in the water, when I was really floating on my own. He looked like Richard Burton. I had studied linguistics and had almost become a computer specialist because of him. He had predicted the information superhighway, the inroads on private life, the immediacy of the Internet, virtualization, cheaper movies, and free music. And this man, so prescient in so many ways, was asking me if I liked women?

I spent some time in the depths of my inclinations, seeking

in that rarely visited darkness to discern what I loved, what I didn't like, what resonated within me (my absence of sexuality notwithstanding), and what kept quiet. I made a complete tour of my being. I looked up at Axel: "Nope, for me it's men." That set him off: "And just how can you be so sure about that if you've never tried anything else?" I pointed out that I had just reviewed the possibility there, right in front of him, while I was deep in thought. Hoping to deflect an objection, I asked if he, personally, could go with a man. To my amazement, he allowed as how if it was only a question of penetrating a man, or receiving a sloppy kiss from one, he probably could. Worst case, closing his eyes, he'd simply imagine that the man was a woman. He admitted that it would be better if the man had long hair and wore nail polish.

We said good-bye out on the sidewalk. A little punch to my shoulder: "Listen, let me say this. . . . I'm truly sorry, in this city abounding in women, that you can't desire a single one of them." Did he know that he was talking about himself?

Gordon had the apartment next to mine. Always in a suit. In finance. The concierge and I had both been surprised that a bourgeois couple had chosen to live in an artist's studio. On Palm Sunday, his wife, a petite woman made nondescript by a hunting jacket, hung a green branch on their door. They had three grown children who no longer lived with them but visited on Sundays, sullen and sinister. I never heard laughter, even though I listened. The aroma of roast leg of lamb reawakened my nostalgia for a family. After the fine meal, the children left, racing down the staircase. Escaping, basically.

One night, coming home after a movie, I found Gordon in front of his door, sitting on the floor in his pajamas, next to his doormat. He had stripped the leaves from the green branch, which had dried out months ago, and crumbled them to powder. Not a happy camper. I figured he'd forgotten his keys and that the door had slammed shut behind him, perhaps when he'd taken down the garbage. The absurdity of his predicament had shaken Gordon's habitual reserve, and I easily persuaded him to come inside my apartment with me.

You think people will have some scruples about unburdening themselves, but not at all. That evening, Gordon had tried to approach his wife. They had separate bedrooms. So what Gordon had done was: he had knocked on the matriarchal door, he had entered, he had lain down on the bed next to the female body, tenderly but without asking any permission. *She* had shrieked loudly, which I would have heard if I'd been home. Keyed up on account of the shrieking and because something was finally happening, Gordon had pressed his case, namely by pressing his head in between his wife's thighs and grunting. She had advised him not to be an idiot and had launched a kick at random that connected with Gordon's shin. "Since that's the way it is," Gordon had cried bitterly, "I'm leaving!" She had leapt briskly from the bed before he did, opened the front door, and ordered him out. Although his wife's nightgown had been hanging open, on his honor Gordon had had no other choice but to leave.

He was distressed at having imposed his disaster on me and wanted to leave. But really, he couldn't just keep leaving. I made him sit back down on my sofa. For the last five years his wife had refused to let him touch her. She had pointed out to him that the male body is repulsive. That last time, five years earlier, he standing naked before her, they had examined the question together. He'd been forced to admit the weirdness of the masculine physique. She had been specific: Gordon's body wasn't more disgraceful than any other man's, but it had the misfortune of being closer, that's all. These revelations had mortified Gordon, who had already endured being abandoned as a child by his mother to the custody of his father. A psychoanalyst to whom Gordon had gone for guidance had led Gordon to understand, whether through masculine solidarity or Freudianism, that too much was too much, and that he could remake his life. After an endless year of famine and introspection, Gordon had suggested a separation to his wife. She had refused. Instead, she had organized a daily routine from which all contact between them was banished. After five years, she touched Gordon only to remove, say, a loose thread from his suit. Sometimes he stuck one on, on purpose.

Gordon went with prostitutes. He was aware that they felt no desire for him. Perhaps they at least somewhat desired the setting, the nice hotel, the mystery, Gordon's personal cleanliness? He went so far as to consider the audacious and up-front contempt of these tarts as one of their advantages. He'd started one evening in Nice. He was in the elevator, going up to the seventh floor. The door had opened on the third floor, revealing a sumptuous creature posed hand on hip in a handsome caramel-colored leather coat. Without making a move, she had announced in French, with a strong Slavic accent: "It's shearling." The words, rather than the woman, were what had captivated Gordon. The elevator door was closing; she still hadn't moved. Adieu. Nothing in Gordon's permanently crushed state could have given him the strength to express a desire. That was when, in extremis, in a demonstration of surprising strength, the woman had held the door open with one finger. And stepped in. It was clear that she was going up for him. Not for one second did he think about his wife. The life his body led no longer had anything to do with the Parisian studio. He had just spent five years without fondling anyone but himself. For five years he'd generated his own pleasure, alone in his bed, off on a voyage. He had lived off the generator, dreaming of love, and why not his wife's love. . . . And we know that love, it's so difficult. That sexuality should return to him as the tawdriest of vices—that was the unexpected aspect of the story. In the hotel room, the shearling coat had slid to the floor. He stared at it, entranced. And she noticed that, the whore. She remembered the elevator, remembered that this man loved words, and she'd spoken some to him. This man who had one last problem of knowing whether his body was capable of feeling desire—this man was stupefied by the ease with which it happened. She tossed words to him, like succulent little fish tossed to a sea lion, and he leapt at them openmouthed in a state of indescribable happiness. Besides, she had something in her eyes, of course. *Yes* to a hint of darkness, to availability. Which she demonstrated without taking offense at anything. He dared to ask for things without a name. Draping the magic coat back around her shoulders, she had announced the price of her performance. Exorbitant though it was, Gordon thought it quite reasonable.

No man had ever told me about frequenting prostitutes. I had to become that neutral individual before anyone would speak openly of it to me.

A s soon as she met a man, she would call me to offer up the freshest of scoops, bearing as they did on the man sleeping in the next room. The phone would ring in the early-morning hours and even though I knew it would be her, I'd feel a twinge of dread. I always learned of deaths at dawn.

We had this ritual where she would say, "I hope I haven't woken you up," and I would lie and say no. In a comical, muffled voice she would ask, "Can you hear me, there?" I could, in the quiet of my bed. She was obliged to mutter, so as not to disturb the sleeper nearby. If they were in a hotel, she'd call from the bathroom. Why go to such trouble? She never awakened anyone but me. After a few moments she would forget to whisper and speak in her normal voice. Back in the bed, her partner slept on. Through what miracle would a man have managed to emerge from sleepy limbo after what she swore to me they'd been up to? It was already dumbfounding that she herself was even able to hold a conversation.

Each man performed better than his predecessor: "With him, it was truly a revelation." She'd forget having trotted out that line dozens of times. She'd elaborate upon one episode, then another, and if I did not react, she'd lay a third one out for me. Producing them the way a magician pops rabbits out of a hat. Or she'd use some generality: "We didn't sleep a wink all night." As for me, I thought that if everybody made such noisy love, we'd never be able to hear ourselves think. I'd go into ecstasies to please her. Our ritual required that one person claim to have experienced extraordinary things, and that the other agree (without really thinking so) that the episode was indeed beyond belief. Me, I couldn't imagine going a whole night without sleep.

I don't know if love makes us blind, but I do believe that solitude allows us to see inside people's minds. In connection with my job, I was waiting to meet one of Pierre's friends. A March day, utterly blue. Perched on a parapet in front of La Grande Arche, the monument in the business district of La Défense, I picked around in my cone of roasted chestnuts. Men and women were coming and going out of subterranean passages; the ones who were late had their shoulders hunched, while the early ones stared anxiously at the beckoning mall and shivered in the shadow of the towers. The arch was overhead, basking safe and sound in the sun. That should have been a hopeful sign, but instead of making me feel secure, the massive power of the architecture just added to the overkill of the whole thing. It was strange to think that each of these human beings before me—the shabby ones, the short fatties, the old wrinkled ones, the blubber-lippers, the dreadful dressers, the ones sporting terrible ties, the pallid souls— might be the object of someone else's desire. I imagined some sort of medical imagery showing all these people confronted by their own sexuality, which certainly highlighted my own futility, so I granted the image some measure of solemnity. It's easy to admit that others aren't wrong when one is so happy *not* to think the way they do. I felt far, far apart from the crowd. . . . And if I stayed there, drinking it all in, it was because I needed to be there, viewing the examples of these automata caught up in society. Without reality, there can be no heady escape from it. You have a handicap—and then you turn it into an aptitude. Like that actress using sign language on television: "I'm gifted: I'm deaf."

A passing man met my eyes, which was quite a feat, since they'd become slippery, hard to catch. He slowed down, turned around a few yards past me. A gray suit. So nervous his briefcase was jiggling against his leg. The pigeons looked like his little gray brothers. He bought some chestnuts. The Indian vendor offered to warm them up one by one on the grill. He agreed. The briefcase sat tamely at his feet. And he, that man, lit a cigarette, turned toward me. His covetous desire was spoiling my beautiful day. I'd have to find another spot.

Stan was gay; you couldn't miss it. His startling beauty. The way he looked when seated: arms and legs placed just so, one atop the other in a mikado pose. The distinction of his interlaced fingers. The magnificent creases in his trousers. His humor. At thirty-nine, a life spent keeping his own sweet distance.

He used to take me dancing, except that we wouldn't be taking to the floor. We preferred to case the joint. Wearing our impeccable white pants, our personal lavender scent, and our difference, we'd collapse onto a slightly malodorous banquette and I'd listen to him describe the others, the normal people on display before us. Stan was a stylist. Others search through the archives of fashion; he loved to marvel at the inelegance of the hoi polloi. He studied them, and his poetry rose above it all in the end, a chemical reaction. I used to wonder what clothing and a sense of humor were helping him forget. He had been HIV-positive, but now he acted as if he weren't anymore. He didn't talk about it. You had to know him well to understand what lurked behind his terror of colds, his extraordinary aggravation over any kind of skin irritation. Once, limping after ten days of seclusion with an episode of bursitis, he had reappeared at the Café Marley in a formfitting blazer, holding a cane topped with a death's-head pommel.

Some evenings he collapsed on my neck. His milky blue eyes flowed like an ointment into my soul, and each time he cackled guiltily, each time he told me what perfume I was wearing, persuading me that he'd come so close simply to confirm it. I'd have sworn up and down—in spite of what people said about Stan and his vices, about some mind-boggling word tattooed on his penis—that like me he was only a spectator of sexuality, someone above all that. I remember a girl in a lemon-yellow miniskirt and black tank top, with a crown of platinum hair. She made straight for him—she'd recognized him or else knew him, whatever—and he'd gripped my arm: "Why, it's Maya the Happy Honeybee! But what's she buzzing around *me* for?"

Toward three in the morning, two assistants would come get him: "Stan, we're moving on. Come along with us, now." Which meant: places in the night where my femininity no longer belonged. He would promise not to leave me. He wanted to spend his life with me. Why didn't we get married? The others were growing impatient: "C'mon, move it." Stan acted as if he took orders from no one, but he would get to his feet, straighten his clothing, try to do up the shirt off which he'd popped a few buttons. He liked to show me his torso. Carried off by his assistants at four a.m., he'd wave his arms at me and flap his hands like someone being torn away from a dear relative.

One December 25, I was reading Antoine de Saint-Exupéry's *Night Flight* in the emergency room of the Hôpital Cochin. I'd stepped on a pin, the tip of which had broken off in my foot, and they were going to remove it. I was waiting, and about halfway through the book. The orthopedist had come into my cubicle with two female students; he had verified the position of the foreign body on the X-ray and had checked the instruments laid out on the medical instrument cart. After slipping on his surgical gloves, he'd been summoned to a more serious case. He'd asked where I would put my pain on a scale of one to ten. I'd said two, not wanting to be a burden.

The cubicle door was open. Out in the corridor, worried people were searching for other worried people. They'd ask who I was. They'd go away disappointed. A male practical nurse wearing a Santa Claus cap tried to escort a street bum back to the reception desk, telling him, "No, I can't possibly give you any ninety-proof alcohol. No, not even a swallow, old boy." He had his hand flat against the bum's back, and with each step they took, the little bell on the cap jingled. A woman with a bandaged head, lying on a stretcher next to a wall, had just been brought in and wanted some water. A hospital attendant, a young woman from Martinique, kept telling her that a doctor would have to decide. The woman would reply that she was a patient. The attendant would answer that patients had to be patient and that *that* was how you could tell they were patients. A man farther off was screaming. Perhaps the orthopedist was doing something to him before taking care of me.

In *Night Flight*, the pilot, Fabien, is exhausted from battling a storm. The shifting winds keep his hands clenched on the stick. Where the weather report had predicted smooth flying, he sees nothing but roiling sky with no horizon. The copilot keeps asking if they're in trouble. They've lost radio contact with the control tower. Fabien is surrounded by difficulties. The clouds are massing together. Fabien has never wanted to plunge into the darkness; he's tough, but he's at the end of his tether. Through a sudden gap in the clouds he catches a glimpse of starry sky and tells himself he can make it through. And he climbs. He flies higher, up over the clouds.

Late that night, the orthopedist and the two students appear again: it's my turn. One of the young women notices *Night Flight*: "I read it in school." I say, explaining that I've just finished it, that it was marvelous: "The pilot escapes from the storm." She corrects me: "Yes, but he dies." Me: "Oh really? He dies?" I hadn't realized. Her: "Yes, of course, he hasn't enough fuel left to get down." The orthopedist isn't happy with the necrosis where the needle went in. My body is fighting to expel a foreign body. Well, on this particular point—my not tolerating any further intrusions—my metabolism is definitely up to the challenge. They are taking me off to the surgical unit. The anesthetist apologizes to me in advance; shots in the foot are not pleasant at all. Even though he's been on duty for twenty-three hours, he gets a laugh out of my reply: "That's all right, I have my head in the clouds."

was at the florist's. Dazzled by the poppies in their bucket, I didn't hear the shopkeeper suggest some enormous roses, arrogant but sociable. He wound up waving them under my nose. He stuck them so close they were going to prick me. "That's not what I want, monsieur," I told him. From now on I was saying what I didn't want. Stubbornly, I had taken up a position in front of the poppies. With an ill grace, keeping the roses in one hand, the man had removed a skimpy clutch of poppies from the bucket, five distracted flowers nodding in different directions. He held both the roses and the poppies out to me, so that I could see for myself which was better. Still meeting resistance, he asked, "It's not to give someone, right?" "Actually, it is," I replied. "Ah, so it's to give someone?" he said, for one last try. He wanted at least to put two bouquets together, to make the blooms look more substantial. I agreed with him and announced that in this case I'd take the six bouquets in the bucket. Go figure: he was still upset. "Oh, really, all of them?" Dismay can be so appealing. Such a young man. I said that he shouldn't worry about this gift, I was sure it would be appreciated. This word "gift" had reminded the florist that the flowers really were for a present; I wasn't joking. He rushed to his worktable, heaped with ferns and eucalyptus branches. I had to explain to him that the person to whom I would be giving the flowers did not like foliage. That the person to whom I would be giving the flowers wanted flowers, plain and simple.

n Venice Henrietta had the idea to take us to the Museo
Correr. She had sworn to the children that there was a room
full of weapons and some pictures of ladies in costumes. She
promised sculptures by Canova that would blow us away.

She was right. The sculptures were in the main gallery, at
the entrance: marble reliefs illustrating short allegorical scenes.
Henrietta deciphered what they meant. We listened to her with
half an ear. Knowing wasn't the most important thing; we were
busy discovering. For us, the delicious indifference of those
profiles in stone. For us, the shoulders stretching into arms,
the arms lengthened by fingers, and the tiny feet, the cajoling
bellies, the muscled calves, the silent dances. For us, the drap-
eries, the sandal thongs. The children managed to be patient,
commenting on every panel as if it were a comic strip. The
miracle of the Canovas affected even Carlos, who wanted to
take photos of them and could not understand why a guard
wouldn't let him. As for Henrietta's little daughter, she attempted to touch them. That, too, was out of the question.
Pierre made her step back. She had a tantrum in the middle
of all the tourists. She crouched down in anger at the injustice

of it all, her pretty pale-green dress sweeping the floor. Tears rolled down her chubby cheeks, even rounder now, crammed with words she wasn't allowed to say, full of her own idealism that she had to swallow down. "Liars! Liars!" she yelled at us. "You're all horrible—except for beauty!" At the age of five, a genius. Gathering from our reaction that what she'd said might have been funny, she saw she could either latch on to our mood or shut herself up in unhappiness. As the daughter of Henrietta and Pierre, she chose the first solution. Her mouth lost its square shape. The crisis was over. Calmly, after blowing her nose, she asked her father if the reason no one was allowed to pet the people in white marble was that they were dead. Pierre made some kind of playful response and suggested that it was now time to go see the pictures of the costumed ladies. Pierre's crew cut gave him authority; he worked in the police force. In a few seconds, the group had disappeared.

Only I stayed behind in front of that white humanity, looking longingly at those profiles.

Rue de Rome, Paris. A fat man surrounded by wind instruments in a music store. He was turning a trumpet over and over in his hands as if he were twirling a fascinating six-gun. Those cowboy movies, I never got to watch them all the way to the end when I was little. I always had to go to bed.

Silence in the store when the man fished a mouthpiece from his pocket, fitted it to the trumpet, and brought it to his lips. His cheeks puffed out only a little; there wasn't time for them to look silly. Then there was music: slow, masterfully controlled yet free, with a serenity that had nothing to do with the now-incomprehensible activity out in the street. Four fingers pressing in turn on the valves; four fingers were enough. The embodiment of a caress. The utter suavity of the melody and the conciliatory, melancholy body of this trumpeter compelled a reconsideration of his heftiness, his slovenly, vaguely beige clothing, and, while we're at it, the clumsiness of men in general.

At the end we applauded. Right outside the store, those behind the window who'd heard so poorly clapped their almost silent hands. As for him, he hadn't looked up once and now stared thoughtfully at the trumpet, rubbing his chin. No customer dared go up to him, and neither did the clerk, who was used to this. Gradually the hubbub of voices returned; the man, off in his corner, continued to mull over the vanished melody.

I approached the wizard. Taking imperceptible little steps toward him, I advanced past the clerk, the customers, the keyboards, the electric guitars; I was abreast of the saxophones. He'd stepped aside to let me by. Me: "I wanted to congratulate you." It embarrassed him that I was a woman. The trumpet encumbered him; he looked around for somewhere to set it down, get rid of it. "It's nice," I said, "what you do." He shrugged. "You ever blown into one of these things?" His gruff voice didn't fit with what we'd just heard. He looked me up and down. He demanded a new mouthpiece from the clerk. He fitted it to the trumpet and handed me the instrument: "So try it." A sort of provocation. A command issued by an extremist. I blew into the trumpet: What else could I do? Not a peep came out. "Go on, try again," he said teasingly. I produced an insignificant bleat.

He made fun: "So, it's easy, the trumpet?" And asked, "May I invite you for a drink?"

He felt there were two categories of human beings: men and women. The more privileged caste was satisfied with pleasure: that was the men. In a different, more sentimental caste, the women were getting nowhere. He talked to me about women, beings different from me, whom we could examine together: "They mix up the physical and the emotional." It never occurred to him that this amalgam might be an advantage or a form of heroism. Men had the ability to come without love. Women did not. I asked him how he explained female masturbation, the fact that a woman could come so fast with a sex toy that she'd fall asleep afterward. He refused to believe it was true. I confessed that it was true for me. He was offended: "How would you feel if I talked to you about inflatable dolls? Would you like that?" I countered by saying that in my opinion, an inflatable doll had more emotional resonance than a sex toy. The doll represented a person. The sex toy represented the function. He gripped the table with both hands. I thought he was going to hurl it aside and storm out of the café. Acting as if he had the better line of patter in a job interview, he pointed out that I was not presenting myself very cleverly.

Or very sexily, as though I should be sucking up to get hit on. He'd been unable to establish a friendship with any woman for the past six months. "As soon as I become adoring, they think I'm in love." Even women of a certain age (I didn't dare ask which one), whom the prospect of the void ought to have rendered modest and conscientious, well, no: they had both hopes and pretensions.

He had just finished the book *Men Are from Mars, Women Are from Venus*. He insisted on telling me that this wasn't the sort of book he usually purchased. Faulkner, that was more his style. And Kierkegaard, had I read him? He didn't hear me when I answered yes. In *Men Are from Mars, Women Are from Venus* (once he'd overcome his distaste for leafing through nonsense, of course), he'd seen certain things confirmed. Men have an instinct for domination. Men remain the hunters they were as cavemen. Men have permanent desires. Constant ultimatums from *here*—and with one finger, one of those that had held the trumpet, he pointed to a place on his body.

Art was another area where he let no woman approach him.

A friend from work was in despair one day. Men? She no longer even understood how to meet them. "There aren't any," she complained. I tried to open her eyes. I talked to her about Stan; she asked whom I thought I was fooling. We started watching for men to pass by in the street. We didn't see any. Was it some faculty that we'd lost, or the bleeding wound of an entire civilization?

We discussed what we'd do if we spotted one. We'd go right up to him, without waiting for him to think of it first. Unless by some stroke of luck, seduced by our mere existence, he were to stop by our table on his own. She added that we were dreaming: it would never happen. I felt it was possible because, I suggested, the man might be someone wild, extravagant, cavalier, a kind of living god. "A god? From where?" she countered. "A god in the absolute sense," I explained. Ah: if I meant some kind of premium-quality demiurge, she'd go along with that. We considered what his profession might be. Running through the ones she was familiar with, she came up with architect. But we'd both known a few architects who'd had nothing godlike about them. More racking of brains. She started up again: "Aren't any. I told you." I fought back against her defeatism, even going so far as to discover the gift of this god: "He's an orchestra conductor. At night his back rises and falls for music and for love." She agreed with me and wasn't as sad as before. She coaxed more of what made him special out of me: "He's a tall, world-famous Chinese guy globalized by his traveling and his devotion to Mozart. He goes everywhere in the world, he comes on to women, but it's only a distraction, a hobby; he's really looking for one in particular. He'll recognize her. Of all creatures, the one he prefers walks with confidence; her strides give breadth to the street, she floats within her garments, the elegance of her body can be deduced simply, from her delicate joints, and she's ripe for the plucking. He's closing in. . . ."

I'd cured the absence that was eating at her. She was fulfilled and I, empty. She could not speak anymore. She was gazing at the Chinese man. I had given birth to him.

A simpler soul than I, she was meeting him in her mind's eye.

She was walking in front of me on rue d'Assas, and her clothes swayed, skimming the ground; they were that sandy color between beige and gray, the color of turtledoves. I was following her. It was as if wherever she went, I was going that way too, and vice versa, and I kept my distance as best I could, spellbound by our differences. What did we have in common, this woman and I? I was wearing a bright-red dress cut low in front, and my white sandals with heels made my feet look beautiful, or at least I hoped so. She was a different story. The dress was beyond austere, with layers. A wimple covered the neckline. I wondered, what was it for? Because the cloth framed her partly hidden face in such a way that it was more presented than concealed; compared to mine, her self-effacement seemed debatable. Which of us was the more noticeable in the blazing hot street in July? I thought her outfit was meant to be a warning: "Don't touch me." A permanent admonition of capital importance, to be renewed every day, to protect herself from desire.

She leaned down in front of a bakery, her face reflected in the window. That face. Asceticism molded her temples, flowing in abnegation down her cheeks. There was no primordial tension within her but rather a vague quietude. A shelter, yes: she had one. I recalled the pointless words of the people of God. The allegories, the songs: "Spread the news far and wide / Send it throughout the land / We shall all meet on the other side / For God is now made man." Those things in which I did not believe, things that would be of no help to me. Destiny must have been a simple thing for the young nun who pushed open a door and disappeared, leaving me only a glimpse of a cloister that was proof against all temptation.

VI

saw his eyes as blue; he swore to me they were green. I saw him as handsome; he coughed in amazement and assured me: handsome, no, *that* he'd never been. I thought him masterful; he got up from the table just to deflate my illusion. Standing there, he sighed, letting his shoulders droop. When he sat down again next to me, surrounded by people with whom he no longer had any connection, I loved him.

He tried to avoid compromising himself, tried to play the fellow who couldn't care less about being someone's crush. But over and over during that dinner, his curiosity impelled him to look at me with disconcerted eyes. I put everything that wasn't my body, everything that knew how to fly, into my smile. Because I didn't know how to awaken anything else. I murmured funny things to him. I found his simple laughter ravishing. He couldn't get over having been noticed. He was honest enough not to hide his surprise. Maybe he'd never had an adventure like this before. Despite his astonishment, he allowed me to press my point; he put up a gentle front of understanding, someone who at least agrees to think about it. My fingers grazed his wrist; he took my hand in his and didn't let go again.

In the street, I looked up at the clusters of chestnut-tree flowers, leaning my head back while he nibbled at my neck. I was practically naked above the waist, backed up against a car. With his hips, through our clothing, the man went through the motions of what I'd given up. I'd forgotten the precision of this human pendulum. Desire and its manifestations, I shouldn't lose sight of them. Would I be ridiculous? I would. Already, my body was bolting doors in strategic places. Already, shutters were slamming closed as my security system went into gear. Those famous gestures we never forget, the ones we know before we learn them, where were they? Fear kept climbing up my back, clinging with kitten claws. My leaden arms discouraged the man's caresses, blocking his every attempt. He couldn't think of anywhere else to touch me. What should I have done? I was annihilated by inertia. How do other people cope? You would have thought that in a burst of temerity, this accidental lover just might teach me how. He tried again to draw me close. I shoved him back against a chestnut tree. Those jellyfish stings you'd swear had healed? If you go back into the sun too soon, they reappear, horrible, intact, and olive green. And the man was helpless; really, no one could have done anything at all that night to quiet the despair going crazy in my heart. I loved no one.

can testify that one can feel pain from love without feeling any love. Looking at myself in the mirror the next day, instead of my body, my face, and the hands I was wiggling to make sure of this, *I no longer had anything but my indefinite human person*. Once the mirror of my friends, overnight I had become a vague, blurry shape, the kind you see behind a stained-glass window. My being had lost the solidity of things: I felt transparent, as though I saw objects right through me.

I sat down, my head in my hands. I was condemned. I would jump off a bridge into the Loire where the water is the most dangerous. I would let myself fall from the top of a dam. I would not be able to live anymore because I realized that physical life is something that someone else gives you. Long after childhood, long after your mother, someone must stubbornly repeat, "These are your eyes; this is your back; here, your hands, your eyelashes, your teeth, your skin, little gold flecks in your irises, your freckled back, your arm is a javelin. . . ." Otherwise, you don't know.

Where were they, the delightful baths of yesteryear? I suspected that from now on, if my body emerged from the foam,

I'd send it back underwater. I would have a surprising grip for someone of my size. I'd keep my body under wraps until I had drowned it, paralyzed it with dejection. Let's not talk about it anymore. I would not enjoy having it drift back up as if nothing were the matter. The bastard had locked itself up tight under the chestnut trees.

That afternoon my telephone rang. An unknown number; I didn't pick up. Afterward I listened to the message: a man's voice. At first I didn't understand a word—the voice was strained too thin: my anxiety was wadding it in cotton, shutting it down in a flash with my usual expertise. A few words: ". . . unexpectedly . . . yesterday . . ." And, more distinctly: "I wondered if you'd like to go with me tonight to the Jeu de Paume museum?" Later that evening, a last, shrewd inquiry: "Were you able to break free?"

'd piled my books up and taken them down to the garbage. Their contents served no purpose. All they did was tell stories. These works I had read—Elsa Morante, Gabriel García Márquez, Camus, Jim Harrison, Virginia Woolf, Aragon, and Éluard, whose words I'd drunk in: "You are the great sun who goes to my head when I am sure of myself"—they were for people ready to believe anything. I'd gotten lost in the dream of things. After searching for so long, I had found my refuge: a jail. My integrity was a suit of armor. Or, how atrocious: I was armor on the inside, with my deceitful flesh on the outside.

I'd made as many trips as there were treasures in my home. No matter that I was young; I had the back of an old woman. I stepped into the elevator woefully bent over. Those books, I held them in my arms, resting my chin on them, and it was awful how much I still loved them as I bore them to the sacrifice. It made me so sad to destroy my riches. I moaned. There is complacency in complaining. But shit, I'm allowed to hang on to that.

Piles of books lined up around the garbage cans: the nauseating corral contained my impossible expectations. Closing the door on them, I felt as if I were leaving an entryway where a night-light was still burning. I almost went back to stomp on it. Exasperating, this survival of art. And what if I stayed behind there? What if my place were there as well, amid the trash? Back in my apartment, I collapsed onto my sofa, if not relieved, at least more honest. I wasn't lying to myself anymore with literature.

I was dropping off to sleep when my doorbell rang. It was one of my neighbors, with books in her arms. As in a nightmare, I thought she was bringing them back to me. No: she wanted to thank me. "And it's even better than the library, too, because here, they're the books you've loved." Off she went to the stairs, holding tight to the fortune I hadn't known how to make use of.

She'd brought a brioche and was eating it eagerly. At the age of eighteen, Tosca had come to Paris from the Balearic Islands to study Chinese. I'd known her as a child and had promised her parents I'd keep an eye on her.

She'd turned up at my door quite early one morning without any idea that I had just stumbled so badly. She had to talk to me. She was incandescent, indignant, her lovely neck tense. Whatever she had done the previous evening, it must have given her a violent shock. She'd come to tell me that she had chosen a path, the same one I had. The thoughtful consideration she'd offered men as a gift, the delicate attentions from her hands, had they been graciously received? No. The boys had treated Tosca's "yes" as well-worn foreplay. Never content. Never satisfied. They'd proposed appalling variations for their romping under the pretext that the rest hadn't counted. The rest: the gift Tosca had made of her person. Tosca's precious youth. She was nineteen. These clods thought they had a right to splendor. "You can't imagine the things I heard." She no longer wished to make herself available.

That saddened me. Besides being exceptionally beautiful,

Tosca was intelligent. Not content to stick with what she knew. Didn't men see that? If I spoke to her about a book, she rushed to buy it. Two days later she would talk to me about it in a trance. After a year of stuffing herself with ideograms, bewildered by Asiatic complexity, she'd had the courage to set off for three months in Hong Kong on her own. She sent me e-mails that rang out in the night with the special tune I'd given them. And once: "Today, Sophie, a man in the street understood what I said!" Well, that young woman, gifted enough to communicate with a Chinese stranger, brave enough to visit the ends of the earth—whom does she run into in Paris? Jerks. She would have accepted anything in initiation from a true mentor.

"I want to live like you, for art," she proclaimed. She was proud of having taken a stand. The wings on her back crackled with sparks. I didn't say a thing. Suddenly intrigued, she looked all around my living room. "Where are your books?"

No summertime lasts long in Paris, but that year the dog days were dragging on. Whatever was I doing in Montmartre in heat like that? Two in the afternoon. Besides me there were only tourists, forced as they were to be outdoors getting their money's worth. A group from Quebec. The beneficial optimism of their accent. Sidling up to them, I absorbed their good humor. They were heading up to Sacré-Coeur, so I did too.

Once up there, they'd plunged into the basilica, and I'd followed them. Sacré-Coeur may not be an emotionally stirring monument, but inside it was truly cool and refreshing. One passed from summer to eternity. We were all sprinkling holy water on ourselves. Someone kept coming to replenish the supply. The gilded Christ held out his arms to us. It didn't surprise me that his proffered chest, his gesture of infinite welcome, was not vast enough to handle the uncertainties gnawing at me in those days. What's more, I strolled around, studying the barrel vaults, the pilasters, the buttresses, and the benches, none of which managed to affect me. Near the booth, signs announced that confessions were heard there all day long. The confessional, and a priest in the darkness. I'd read once in a newspaper that for years many criminals, the ones below boulevard de Rochechouart, would come to this basilica to unburden themselves when they'd killed someone. They'd pour things out for a few minutes before heading back to the carnage.

The priest on his stool—I was sure he saw me as a customer. The round toes of his shoes reminded me of the childishness of Disneyland. I thought I saw him wearing Mickey Mouse's white gloves in the shadows, but it was only his chubby fingers. And yet it occurred to me to turn to this man of God. To confess to him how fear was paralyzing me. I could have talked to him about sins I no longer knew how to commit. I remembered the details Father Mario used to demand in the church of Notre-Dame de Grâce de Passy, in the sixteenth arrondissement. At the time I was already inventing little touches for the sins I hadn't committed, to please him. My present failings: Were they something I could put into words? Could I say, "Father, it pains me to be more innocent-as-a-lamb than your flock"? What would he think, this director of conscience, of my incurable purity?

What could a God do who might have the same problem I did?

found it on the sidewalk. In a navy-blue box, long enough to hold a checkbook, gold clasp, Hermès. The Béarn model. Two months earlier I'd had to pass on getting myself one. And now, so empty that it looked new, it trembled in my hands, a compensation for my fate. The consolation prize. There was no shop nearby, of course, no place to leave a phone number, no prominent ledge where I could leave the wallet. If I took it, it would be mine.

At the police station, I reluctantly handed the wallet over to a policewoman, and so ungraciously that you might have thought that I myself had swiped it and now, remorseful, was giving it back. The woman had me sit down. You couldn't tell whether the officer was examining the wallet out of curiosity or professional conscientiousness. She set it down between us, a shared possession. With the paranoia I'd admired in Inspector Columbo, she concluded that the thief had been illiterate: if he'd known how to read, he would have known what "Hermès Paris" meant; any idiot could have figured that out. I couldn't have agreed more. She took down a short statement: I stated that I had found the wallet, boxed, navy, gold clasp in the form of an H, marked "Hermès Paris" inside, at the corner of rue Royale and rue Saint-Honoré. I stated that the wallet was empty. We checked together to be sure. She told me that the wallet would be sent to the Lost and Found Department of the Ville de Paris. I made a joke about it being a treasure. No, she told me, a treasure was something found by chance, but it had to have been hidden or buried. "Whereas with you, it was neither hidden nor buried," she insisted, a trifle more suspiciously. "No," I lied, "my case is nothing like that. . . ."

The poor boy, lying on the sidewalk on the bridge, Pont Alexandre III. A man in a short-sleeved shirt was asking onlookers not to come any closer. He didn't claim we had to give the wounded man air; he just kept us at a distance by holding up the flat of his hand. We milled around where he said to stay. As soon as he dropped his arm, nosiness took over and we drew closer. It wasn't our fault: it was to see a dead person. We'd all realized that there was no more hope left in that body. Our impression of the young man's abdomen rising and falling slowly was from our being alive and moving, whereas he had the stillness of stone. A jacket covered his feet. If it belonged to the man in shirtsleeves, that gave him another snippet of authority to make us move back.

People tilted their heads to interrogate the inert face, protected by the boy's long blond hair, some of it spread out around his head like those awful suntan reflectors. All we could see was the lower part, the jaw. And the young man's livid chin, the tender mouth, inspired thoughts of repentance. There were twenty of us watching on the bridge for the fire department's rescue team; they were coming for us, too, and would chase us away. In the meantime, the man in shirtsleeves was there next to the body to defy us. Newcomers wanted to know what had happened. When anyone asked if it was serious, the man didn't look at the person's eyes but slightly higher, at the forehead, the skull, addressing the person's faculty of judgment. Everyone was coming up against the man in shirtsleeves. They'd notice the boy's hand: too white. They were getting bolder. It was demoralizing.

The ambulance arrived, and a stretcher. The firemen bent down; they straightened up. They exchanged a few words with the man in shirtsleeves. He wasn't a doctor but a cook in a restaurant on place de l'Alma. An hour earlier he'd been crossing the bridge and seen the young man get hit by a car, sail through the air, land, and shoot like a projectile for ten yards headfirst right into the railing, and that was it. The firemen seemed perplexed, so the man pointed to the place in the street where the accident had occurred and showed the trajectory of the body. To make things clearer, he went over and picked up the jacket lying across the young man's feet. He was wearing Rollerblades.

VII

An enigma: Carlos, wild-eyed, on boulevard Saint-Germain. Wearing a raincoat even though it was 84 degrees Fahrenheit, according to the display screen outside the pharmacy. He couldn't believe that I hadn't heard the news: he was no longer living at home. He'd already had Henrietta on the phone, and Pierre, the gang from Hydra, those in Basel, and even the swingers. So he warned me: "If it's to stick your nose in too, forget it." He was camping out in a cousin's pied-à-terre—"It's like a hospice"—on rue de Beaune. "I can't manage to swallow anything," he explained, as if this information justified his corrosive derision. Back on avenue Raymond Poincaré, Vionne and the children were cursing him. He was the one who had brought up the subject of leaving. It wouldn't have been running off forever, just a few days away, a breather. He'd suggested it to Vionne one morning in their living room bathed in sunshine, arms open wide, in a carnival-barker mode, something positive, a bit of mischief. Yes, why not: a little love game. Vionne had almost been tempted. Except that during the day she'd discovered his valise hidden away in the wardrobe, with his favorite outfits already packed. Home again after work, Carlos couldn't deny the premeditation. Furious at being called on the carpet for ten folded shirts in an assignation kit, he'd stormed out. His youngest son had sent him a long e-mail: "The reason you gave to Mama is disgusting." And me: "The reason?" And him: "Ah, yes, the reason." He was tired the way someone is who has to keep repeating himself. "I don't want her anymore, you understand?" Even I found that argument pathetic. My enormous prejudice. "So what did you say to her, to Vionne?" He shrugged. "You're all incredible! I told her the truth. How could I have lied to her? With love, you can always get out of a bind because you can't see it, but getting a hard-on, or not, you can't wriggle out of that; might as well be frank about it."

It would be a mistake to believe that Carlos was possessed by some passion or other, for he would rather have gone on with a de-eroticized Vionne in mutual tenderness. Alas, the plan to be at least affectionate with her had not worked out. For months Vionne had taken every kindness from Carlos as a sign of amorous renewal and later attacked him lustfully in bed. He had thought about going with other women, just to see if that might reignite him, a sort of makeup class. Alas, again he was a limp rag with hookers. To disengage himself gradually from Vionne without her taking too much notice, he must have had to leave his balls behind, as a sort of security deposit, so it was no go. I'd been wrong to be contemptuous of Carlos's vulgarity: it livened up the street. He didn't see that

I admired him. "You think I'm a lousy runaway?" It strangled him to talk. I discovered that men have few people to whom they can open their hearts. That they're poorer than we are. Their feelings, when they have to swallow them like pride, turn into gags.

During the day, at the beach, I would doze under a cane awning. In the evening I'd go lie down on a rustic table in the center of a white tent. Life outside went on with its unreal sounds, while I was naked. Before massaging me, Pajane would dribble lukewarm oil onto the top of my skull, and that oil would flow down the back of my neck to my shoulders. With his free hand (the other held the cruet), Pajane would help the oil along until it reached the wooden table. His touch proved to me that there is a shape to our bodies. Instead of sketching out some music in the air, the contact taught me my boundaries, my contours. A woman in clinging silk jersey understands what that dress contains. Dreamily, she verifies herself. Here the miraculous garment was the hand. My oily head fell against Pajane's impeccable white kurta. When I was loath to soil it, he was the one who pressed my head back against him. He pulled on my spine as if to unkink it forever. A little faun destined for delight had been crouched waiting inside me, having hidden under a chest of drawers during my great invasions. Now the faun was coming back to life.

To indicate that I should lie down, Pajane touched two

fingertips to the end of the board, by an invisible pillow. The two fingers on my back or my belly: I was to turn over. He slathered me with so much oil that when he massaged me afterward, the most prominent parts of my body were sliding around on the table, and my feet would bump into his pelvis. I didn't dare open my eyes except when I was on my stomach, with my face fitted into a special hollow on the board that ensured the correct alignment of the cervical vertebrae. In that position I could see Pajane's perfect feet, the pink nails, the white pants rolled up around his exquisite ankles. I decided that I should always have preferred handsome men. I did not admire these marvels for long, because Pajane would grab my skin—I was an obedient greyhound rather than a Dalmatian bitch—and I would go back under my eyelids.

Or he would stand facing me as I sat on the table and pull me tight against the kurta while my legs hung on either side of his hips. Grasping each of my shoulder blades with one hand, he would gently move them apart. I could feel my back open and crows fly out. And he would let me go. In a stupor, I would try to make out his face and encounter only bristling eyelashes edged with light.

My single thought each morning was to get to the masseurs' tent early enough to reserve Pajane. I was becoming more supple. In the water, my new, telescopic neck stretched out with the slightest swim stroke. A single movement propelled me five yards forward.

During my stay in Goa, I never heard him say a single word, even in his own language with the other masseurs. Until the last evening, when I told him in English—on the off chance—that I was leaving the next day. He had his back to me; he turned around. That oil-soaked kurta . . . Slender, with black eyes, he had the teeth of a happy man. In two words, a sage can teach you for the rest of your days.

He spoke in English.

"Necessity body."

Bombay, the plane home. My seat near the window. The Indian baggage handlers on the tarmac; our luggage brought up and tumbling off the carts; the handlers passing the bags by hand one to another. The things that link people together. In the plane, on the ground, it's the same—the human family. A man in sky blue. He'd gotten on the plane pushing two children ahead of him. One hand on the hair of each child. This gesture hypnotized me. He tapped them on the head: they so young, he so tall, a basketball player in love with his small basketballs. Who had adored me like that since my parents? The man's seat was next to mine, the children in the row in front of us. Someone had offered to change seats with him, so they could all sit together, and because the children were already quite boisterous. The man had declined the offer, pointing to his two scamps and telling us, "I've never seen these two before in my life." Their little faces exploded with joy at this paternal naughtiness.

Kneeling on their seats, turned toward us, the kids waited expectantly for the father's sallies before takeoff. "We should say good-bye because we're all going to die," predicted the father in a tone of somber confidence. The little ones were obviously addicted to this sort of thing. They started talking to me right away. They'd just been in a village in southern Goa called Cortalim, they lived in Paris, they'd seen some dolphins. The father said nothing, leaving these expert little goons to ask me my name, and if I was alone and why was that, and if I knew Cortalim, and how old I was. Everyone should get the chance to travel with such monkeys. But they sat back down in their seats surprisingly quickly and became models of discretion, absorbed in perusing the available films.

After they fell silent, the man examined me. "I don't know where I would go on my own," he announced, without specifying if he was talking about traveling or going through life. He scrutinized me, with the idea of getting somewhere. It was impossible to know whether he was playing or if he was daring, on a whim (as can happen), to be frank. That sky blue was a seersucker suit. He smelled of mint.

The overhead monitor showed us flying over Afghanistan. Without warning, this father of two, wearing a wedding ring, practically laid his chest across me to look out the window. Now, first, it was pitch-black out, and second, the shade was down. There was nothing to see. Instead of Afghan mountains, he could contemplate only plain gray plastic. Incomprehensible, this man lying on me so that he could catch a glimpse of nothing. He was so close that I could feel his pulse, his chest as he breathed against my abdomen. I saw a profile like those of Canova's heroes, along with the mischief inscribed in the fine lines on his temples. Settling back into his seat he observed, with remarkable aplomb, "It's cloudy." I, too, leaned toward the closed shade, where there were only dreams. And I announced confidently, "It'll clear up." His mockery and mine, head-to-head the whole trip.

In Paris, waiting for our luggage by the baggage-claim carousel, he shook my hand. "It's too bad," he muttered. The children were playing around his legs, like big links in a chain.

This body cracked open by the massages—thanks to what convoluted thought process did I take it off to yoga when I got back to Paris? The class was held in a room with a skylight; one simply signed up and paid, selected a cubbyhole, and took a mat from a shelf, all actions that did not require saying a word to anyone. A shy complicity with the other students served as a connection. Besides, some people never bothered even with that. They unrolled their mats with blind eyes, already in an autistic solitude of performance as they prepared for the exercises.

The teacher materialized before us. Pale, he possessed as little aura as a cult groupie handing out leaflets. The perfect set of his shoulders set no example. His posture evoked effort rather than harmony. His feet: pale, clean, but orange with calluses. His headband was brown, pink, and mauve. Other colors in his pants clashed even more with those.

The movements to be performed, however, were admirable. The simple action of standing still and dropping your chin while exhaling washed you clean of ugliness. At a certain point, the yoga teacher no longer existed; his callused feet didn't matter anymore. When he addressed you, correcting one of your faults, you heard him from so far away that your breathing let you remain inside yourself. In letting go, the chin brought the neck forward and you felt your nape taking root almost in the small of your back, or even lower. Arched, your neck became that of a thoroughbred. As in Goa. Each part of the body in turn was stretched like this. After twenty minutes you were no longer that former person. Yet no histrionics were involved in these feats of prowess. And again, no connection with your neighbors. You didn't walk around your mat breathing in deeply and beating on your ribs. Those of us who could touch their heads with a foot kept their contentment to themselves. Everything happened between you and yourself. Sometimes, during a difficult exercise or one less suited to your abilities, you had to admit defeat. Yet with your arms hanging by your sides, inert, you still did not become an audience for the others. They continued not to interest you.

No, this discipline was not for me. I had already explored all the solitary pleasures.

Meanwhile, Carlos had been excommunicated. Vionne had gone hunting through the family computer, looking only for suggestive e-mails, inspired by the intuition that Carlos might have another woman in his life and that the few days away with the overnight bag had been only the forerunners of more elaborate plans. Love elsewhere. Vionne was not a computer whiz. She had seen the tab "History" on his browser and clicked on it. Beginner's luck: she'd landed on the roster of porno sites the computer had visited during the past month. Of course there was always the real possibility that her son or daughter had been the one to go there, and to her misfortune, she asked them about that. So it was as a family, so to speak, that they had together followed the pathetic trail of Carlos. They had reviewed each video and seen how often—thirty times—Carlos had clicked on "a slut sucks off her teacher for a passing grade." A video so appreciated that it was in the "Favorites" section. That Carlos was an English teacher had given a special piquancy to the visuals; that he hadn't even tried to cover his tracks emphasized the cruelty of his psychopathology.

I was one of the few people still speaking to him. He had only men left on his side, and even they hid that fact. Pierre would see him nowhere but in a bar off in the western suburbs of Paris. I listened to Carlos grieve. He said he was despicable. He was sick to his stomach with regret. On the other hand, I pointed out to him the ignobility of his children's involvement in the holy alliance against him: "That's more serious than what you did." I assured him that everyone has the right to withdraw to a certain sanctuary, a place of vague desires where we all can hole up without hurting anyone. He looked at me as though I'd been drinking. He shook his head, a man for whom it was too late: he had recognized his crimes.

I encountered Vionne in a Monoprix chain store, where she came toward me with her cart so fast I wondered if she meant to ram me. No, she braked a yard away and barked, "You heard about Carlos?" Surrounded by bras, she enlightened me as to the kind of person she'd married.

"Well *of course* he doesn't want me. Dirty stuff, that's what he wants! The children are in shock. Who would want a real woman after gorging on all those horrors? Some guy with a disgusting gut who's supposed to be a college professor has this girl student alone in his office and it's endless blow jobs, blow jobs with the girl on her knees, blow jobs with the girl standing up, blow jobs on that disgusting gut, and there's Carlos, drooling over blow jobs, blow jobs from a girl of twenty, the same age as his daughter!"

She pronounced the term "blow jobs" in a strident voice, as if she felt her shrillness were a distracting sound that helped disguise the dirty word.

"If he happens to contact you," she added, "you could explain to him that love is above such things. It's lucky I ran into you: I wanted to call you so you'd go speak to him, with your high standards."

A bsolutely every site warned that its contents were unlike anything ever seen before. And then, invariably, it offered the same crudeness. Right from the home page, pleasure was yours for the taking, in just the idea of it. Everything was there, on offer. Of course, they did require you to cough up every last little detail about yourself, but really, if you think about it, you'd have to be a simpleton to think that you can exchange such information for access to more sophisticated marvels, imagining that you'll penetrate to a treasure trove. And yet so many people do it. How naïve. Except that this recourse to our naïveté seemed to me like the genius move of the industry. And I understood this: if one has the reflex to go further, it isn't to leave oneself behind, it's to plunge inside oneself. A yoga. The same solitude.

A man told me one day that sex and humor were incompatible. So how to explain the helpless laughter at these images and what these couplings awakened in me? A liberating idiocy was insinuating itself into the neurasthenia of pornography— including the mediocrity of the verbiage, which became attractive. It *had* to be so dumb. The lack of intelligence would have been simply a detail if it hadn't been replaced by a sup-plementary void. It wasn't enough that the look in the actors' eyes betokened no judgment, no understanding, because there was a bonus: *the implication of a superior imbecility.* We all hope to lose our heads. Well, that promise was fulfilled, floating across the faces of the cast, a surplus of guaranteed stupidity that seemed to me like the chief malice, the major naughtiness of this art, even more so than the close-ups of the decisive zones.

I was in front of my computer screen, strafed with desire. An intensity so quickly fulfilled as to be invisible: my hands hadn't left the keyboard, my hips hadn't so much as twitched. Meaning that the thing that happens in the head had gone up to mine, then back down in a jiffy to the spot in question without giving me the time to think about it.

The Minh Chau restaurant, a little place in the Marais. So microscopic that the proprietors passed the plates from the kitchen to the dining area over our heads. Three scattered clients, if such a word applies in such a place, all women and all eating the one and only dish, ginger chicken. Dinner service was over. Standing behind a kind of counter, the two Vietnamese owners, mother and daughter, were amusing themselves commenting on the street action. A rather good-looking man had come in, seen our interested expressions and the mischievous faces of the owners, and gone right out again before they'd even had time to say the kitchen was closed. We found that funny.

Women have the gift of relating to one another. We'd started talking from table to table—about the chicken who'd flown the coop, of course. "We weren't going to eat him," remarked the pretty girl to my right. Gales of laughter, because, on the contrary, that's probably exactly what we'd have done. Nine ways from Sunday. The conversation got going on the fact that men are afraid of our sexual appetites. One of the other customers was from Korea, and in her own country, she was doubtless a discreet and modest woman. In the Minh Chau restaurant, she was here to tell us that with men, the climate of debauch was not up to snuff. Whatever they wanted or did, nothing matched the fantasies she had in mind. The men claimed that her opaque eyelids drove them to distraction, but at the height of their transports, they were as basic as robots. The boyfriend of the other customer, the pretty girl, had begged her to tell him her secret desires. Well, she knew, she just knew that this would be fatal. That she would traumatize him. He insisted so much and for so long that in the end she gave him two or three examples of what she might envision. The least extreme. Notably, she wanted to call him Franco. At which, her boyfriend, the son and grandson of Spanish communists, had frozen disastrously in bed. Learning that his bank had gone bust couldn't have destroyed him any more thoroughly. Even worse: he'd gotten it into his head that these ideas of hers, she'd definitely picked them up through contact with other men, because he simply couldn't see how she could have come up with them herself.

The women turned to me. And what did I have to say? The two Vietnamese ladies were drinking their jasmine tea in Inox glasses, listening to us. I revealed that in my case, it was special: it had been years since I'd stopped making love. They asked me if I missed it; I replied that lately I'd been receiving insinuating vibrations. That I was perhaps awaiting the arms of an accomplice. That perhaps I was keeping still, hunkered down, a sneaky lowlife. The women agreed unanimously: my fantasy was the most incredible one of all.

VIII

At the age of sixty-four, after years of renunciation—a region more distant than solitude—Axel had fallen in love at first sight.

In the Bois de Boulogne, he showed me unusual and surprising trees, a sequoia and a copper beech, as if his revived happiness had made them flourish. His hand met my arm with assurance, made stronger by his resurrection. He had met this woman in Deauville toward the end of the winter, in a light drizzle. That she'd turned up in the boredom of the beach, in Deauville, a place so hated by Axel—who only went there to see his grandson—was simply a miracle. She'd been walking her dog (it could hardly get any worse). She'd passed by without noticing him, whereas he had avidly absorbed the woman's Mediterranean profile, the *Bitter Rice* details reminiscent of that old Italian neorealist film, the long hair parted on the side. To face down the platitude of his sixty-four years, he'd said, "So, not even hello?" She'd turned around. And had surely seen he was daring the impossible. Well, another miracle: she'd been welcoming. She had asked him where *his* was—his dog, given that no one in those parts would have been foolish enough to go out in the rain without an alibi. He'd proposed a grapefruit vodka. The dog had frolicked along in front of them.

And then that woman, back home in Paris, had desired Axel. As unlikely as that seemed to a pessimist who thought his teeth unspeakable and would run down the list of his dilapidations after a drink or two, a woman wanted him. He had objected that a naked man of his age was not a pretty sight. Without batting an eye she'd replied, "It's not supposed to be pretty, it's supposed to be fascinating." He'd gone straight to the doctor for some Viagra. The doctor had prescribed some for him with cries of joy and had escorted him to the door with hearty claps on the back. The Viagra hadn't worked. Axel's anxiety had been stronger than chemistry. He'd been tempted to give up, but not for long. To begin with, instead of having patience with his flag at half-mast, the woman had said, "This can't be. You can't remain like this. It would be a catastrophe for everyone." It was the first time anyone had encouraged him by yelling at him. Axel had considered how much time he had left before real old age set in. He'd remembered something the comedian Coluche had once said: "Sometimes you just have to wonder if there's life before death." And Axel had gone straight to the sexologist. The man was short, round, facetious, and he, too, talked about Axel's penis with beneficial disrespect. In similar cases, this doctor had found it helpful to put the patient on Viagra every day at different times, long enough—it never took long—for desire to understand its power. He was going to try with Axel. And it had worked. One year from retirement, Axel had suddenly felt savage urges when his assistant walked by, a woman who wasn't the one from the beach and who wasn't attractive in any way, except that she was in the vicinity. At ten in the morning, her boss had had to cling to the water cooler so as not to send sailing through the air that file folder she was clutching to her breasts. Within three days he had replaced his anxiety over not getting a hard-on with alarm over not being able to control precisely when he would get one. This disorganized desire made his heart pound. Was he going to have an attack? No, it was longing, longing that was attacking him. Late one afternoon he called the woman from the beach: "I'm on my way." The next morning, he no longer needed any help.

"And me, where's my miracle pill?" I was talking to Henrietta, giving her Axel's good news. Henrietta was selling the apartment where she'd grown up, in the sixteenth arrondissement, and we were waiting together for the man from the real estate agency. During the winter her mother had died of a ruptured aneurysm. We were in the room—such a small one, really—where I'd studied all that Latin and swanned around. . . . My ever-so-faithful friend, who had read *Night Flight* to understand me better, even though she was terrified of planes and storms. The one who'd said one day, "Be quiet, you don't know anything," to one of our classmates who'd ventured to suggest that I wasn't a real woman. My friend who, for me, had been the face of love. I'd been practically a pariah and she'd managed to make me look better, giving the impression that my difference was an oasis in a desert of conformity. What it means, not to be judged! Her condemnations fell only on others: "It isn't nature that abhors a vacuum, it's them, it's society. And society, screw it." Or: "I mean, you ought to know this: here no one is allowed to live in paradise unsupervised. You know what they're like!" Or: "Those others who find you surprising? You'd be surprised, too, at how vindictive they can be: they scream at one another at dinner parties, and that's what they call love!" Or: "You don't live anything they can see, so they think they can set you right. I mean, the pretentiousness of busybodies has always amazed me." She had legitimized each one of my defenses.

"Your pill, it's what's inside you," she'd replied, and had gone so far as to say, "It's what you've got in your eyes." She wriggled uncertainly. What if she'd just gone *too* far? She was wondering if she was opening or closing something. My fears, so terrorizing that a downy feather would make me explode; the radical way in which I knew how to defend myself—that's what she had on her mind. Henrietta: her perspicacity could not stand being blocked by my boundaries, my calcified impasses. It was her job to extricate, from the loam of the past, the treasures that make History possible. Her daily routine: advancing with a headlamp into passages where the dead have lost all hope. She brought the unknown to light. I'd seen her unearth it even on television, a medium she despised. She had done it solely to give her vision of the world a chance.

She was studying my face, wearing affectionate defiance in the corners of her mouth, truly curious to find out what I was capable of hearing. I bore up under her adoration in that childhood bedroom. I was touched; tears welled up and would spill over in the end. What I had inside me. In my eyes. My hint of darkness like a gift from heaven.

Carlos was moving back in with his wife. He had not been able to withstand the resentment of his tribe. After not speaking to him for a time, they had all abruptly and bitterly demanded to see him, as if he were the one boycotting them, when his own desperate appeals, transparently distressed, had gone unanswered for weeks. He saw his children in cafés, which might as well have been prison visiting rooms, given the bars, the impenetrable glass panel that cut him off from his progeny. When he'd leave the café, with the collar of his overcoat turned up to hide his desolation, he could feel eyes staring at him as if he were being stabbed in the back by his own family. He'd turn around to a new and dreadful disappointment: the two teenagers weren't watching him at all. They'd left the table and were on the phone. Probably calling their mother.

To cap it all, a host of realities had hit him hard. His wife had promised that the separation would cost him dearly. With that in mind, Carlos now saw the most innocent expense as an insurmountable burden. It seemed to him that all he did was sign checks, exhausted, in complete dependence. He assured me that it makes you think, money. . . .

In short, the question of longing had lost urgency. And if it did arise, it was as a piece of property belonging to his wife and children. It was for them to decide: Did they long to see him come back home? The situation had reversed itself. He hated his cousin's studio apartment. He couldn't stand men who were moody and he swore he was over all that. Above all, he cursed the devotees of pornographic videos. He never mentioned that his wife had had the indecency to involve the children in their failure. It was always Carlos who was at fault.

His last, somewhat personal doubt concerned his ability to satisfy his wife. But on this point as well he had reprogrammed himself. He was brimming with goodwill. He could even envision some physical reconciliation and would make the effort. Hadn't his wife re-eroticized herself by refusing to be the mate of a pervert? This might become exciting again, his trying to persuade her, after so many years spent with her eagerness versus his boredom. The potential value of his wife, formerly a source of upset and paralysis because of her manic craving for erotic attentions, now rose in his estimation because her animosity kept her off-limits. It was his body talking. . . .

He returned to the fold almost contentedly. Afterward, for a few months, no one could manage to get in touch with him. To whom could he confess that he'd let himself be had? That having allowed his children to get the upper hand, he had lost his ascendancy over them? That instead of letting herself be won over, his wife had offered nothing but recriminations, taking tiny revenges from which she was the first to suffer? To whom could he have confessed that his life was a dismal mess?

That summer, I did not receive many invitations to vacation houses. There were fewer everyone-chips-in potlucks; I was no longer asked to share communal digs. Before disappearing into the stinging tribulations of his marriage, Carlos had revealed to everybody how much I, more than anyone else, had urged him to break free. I had obviously failed but still represented a danger: someone liable to take your husband and preach independence to him, luring him with the heady smell of other possibilities. An irresistible perfume—otherwise, who would have cared? This happened just when I was making myself more feminine day by day. Others had reproached me for my getups these past few years; now they almost missed my baggy clothes. They noticed the intention behind my red nail polish, my shapelier pants, the pumps they themselves had ordered me to buy. They noticed my breasts and my hips and my ankles. The elements of my revolution not only twinkled in the mirrors in which I was meeting myself again, they announced my return to all and sundry. I had a reflection. I was back.

My restless gaze of the past few years had managed to

pass for an eccentricity. Its current steadiness—an index of my resurrection, a boldness that was the stuff of dreams—isolated me more than all my exiles. My solitude had been an infirmity. Today, like a lever, it invigorated my freedom. People stopped pushing me to come on to men like a vamp. Even a come-hither look would have been too much. Instead, they tried to find out if I wanted to have children, and I understood that this not-unreasonable plan implied a companion. It would be a good thing if I settled down now. My friend in Basel, the one whose husband fantasized about my outraged modesty, the one who had persecuted me at Monster Park, now lost her taste for scandal as soon as her husband, having miraculously outgrown his interest in a three-way scenario, set up a rendezvous with me—alone—in Paris, to which I never went.

Walking along the street, I saw nothing but possibilities. It's true: now that I could see men, I saw them all. One at a bakery was fumbling about his person for change. He put his hand in his pants pocket and I had the impression that I was the one feeling around down there in zones of unspeakable silky softness. And I remembered a little girl's toy, a silicone ball. It was from the beginning of my time-out, after my snowy holiday. The kid had placed it in the palm of my hand, promising me that I would find it delightful. Her favorite toy. I'd been struck by the satiny texture of the ball, recognizable anywhere, and had been surprised that a little girl would notice that attractive quality.

'd never told anyone a thing about it. Now and again, from some innocent remarks made by those close to us, I realize how deeply buried our secret is. So much the better. All sexuality should be like that. We had run into each other by chance, I at the wheel of my car, near Les Invalides, while he'd been crossing the street. I'd given him a lift, which seemed the simplest thing to do. And then we'd had to choose *where to,* naturally. Strangely enough, neither one of us had been going anywhere.

Whether the bonds of marriage are sacred or not, I see them for what they are: ties that are woven, and foreign to me. I did not steal that man. I took him in order to take wing. I wanted to begin again with the body. To unfold myself. Open my shoulder blades, as in Goa. And he, he'd guessed that. For months he'd been thinking about it. Whenever he came near my street, he'd refrained from calling me.

We were heading for my place.

He examined my apartment; he liked it.

As if this followed naturally, he asked what would happen if we fell in love, adding that it would be a catastrophe for a great many people. Without mentioning them, we consulted our consciences about those we would be making unhappy.

He stood quite calmly by my bed with a kind of down-to-earth solidity.

I'd warned him: "You know, those years without anything, years of hugging my pillow, caressing poppies, licking marble, indoctrinating myself with fantasies . . . I don't have a private life."

He'd said, "Believe me, private life is not what you do, it's what you don't do."

I'd warned him that I was fearful, skittish, and that it was dishonorable to have lost my mastery of the basic gestures, especially at my age. I'd warned him that I knew by heart the embarrassment of incompetence, and that—good lord, that was all I knew.

He'd said, "When I was six, my brother used to pass his finger over a flame without burning himself. He swore it was easy. For days I watched him swinging his finger through the fire, for days I brought my hand up to the flame, and each time I thought better of it. I suspected my brother of having some secret lotion. He just loved to play tricks on me from his Magicboy Kit. And then, one time I managed to try it. He was right, it was easy, plus you discovered something irresistible about the flame. After that you couldn't stop doing it."

And I went on; I said, "I'm telling you in advance, I'm letting you know: so many daring things just stayed in my head, so many pleasures were not for me, even dancing was as if I were telling lies in space. I'm afraid it will be too much, what I'm thinking of. Watch out: if you make a move, you will be moving toward an uncertain woman."

But he came over, and as soon as I was able, how quickly I put my hand where it hadn't been in a long time, surprised to touch something that reassured me so much.

ABOUT THE AUTHOR
AND TRANSLATOR

Sophie Fontanel is a novelist, essayist, and editor at large at *Elle* France. This is her first book to be published in English. She lives in Paris, France.

Linda Coverdale has a PhD in French literature, is a Chevalier de l'Ordre des Arts et des Lettres, and is the award-winning translator of over sixty-five books. She lives in Brooklyn, New York.